Lisa –

You did a
great job
capturing us
with the Binky story!

Anne Warfield

OUTCOME
Thinking™

OUTCOME Thinking™

Getting Results **Without** the Boxing Gloves

Anne Warfield, CSP

Retrouvaille Publishing
Minneapolis, Minnesota

Anne Warfield, CSP
Impression Management Professionals
7200 France Avenue South, Suite 224
Edina, MN 55435
contact@impressionmanagement.com
www.impressionmanagement.com

Second Edition

ISBN: 0-9672895-0-5

Library of Congress Catalog Card Number: 00-190465

Printed in the United States of America.

07 06 05 04 03   7 6 5 4 3 2

This book is dedicated to

*My husband, Paul Cummings, who has inspired,
encouraged and believed in me always.*

*Our children who soothe me
with their quick smiles and hugs.*

*To my parents, Margaret and Grant Warfield,
who always taught me to believe in myself,
to do my best and to push ahead at all costs.*

Contents

Contents

Acknowledgements

A book like this doesn't happen without a lot of support from others. I would like to thank my editor, Kathryn Hammer, who made sense of it all, and helped package my thoughts. She interjected humor and insight with her comments and headings.

My designer, Jack Caravela, who worked endlessly on formatting the book so it had just the right feel. His unique cover design speaks eloquently yet powerfully.

My husband, Paul, who has always cheered me on. His belief in what we have to offer and the importance of getting this information into your hands has driven me further as a person.

Pam Bosacker, who has spent countless hours typing and retyping this manuscript. Her endless coaching and encouragement kept me spurred on.

And to all my friends and family that have read and reread my manuscript, put in their comments and helped me polish it up. To all of you I say thank you!

Introduction

You try really hard to see the other person's point of view, but sometimes you just wonder if they are brain dead. You can't see their point at all. And you wonder is it even worth the energy to try to think what they may be thinking when it makes no sense to you at all! (Kind of like that last long sentence!)

And you just wish you could communicate so clearly that you would blow the opposition away. That they would just say, "wow" and do whatever you say. Wouldn't that be great?

But we don't live in a perfect world. And we don't have the same experiences nor have we been taught the same values as we grew up. So not every person is going to think like you and yes, you are going to have a lot of miscommunication.

If you want to connect better with others, be more persuasive and experience less stress, this book is for you.

I wrote this book because I noticed that no matter where I traveled, I saw people's need to be liked and respected. Yet I saw these same people engaging in self-defeating behavior: losing negotiations, breaking partnerships and alienating friends due to misunderstandings and miscommunication.

I realized the need for a new way of thinking; a better way to connect with each other. It's time to move out of the "ME" Generation and into the "WE" Generation as we enter the next millennium. An altruistic goal? No, I wrote this book for selfish reasons; I want the people of the world to be better connected for my own sense of security; as a parent who wants the best world for her children; as a boss who needs to support her staff; and as a friend who values others in her life.

The premise of my book is simple: the more skilled you are at clearly stating your position without offending others, the more positive your results will be. Not only do you accomplish more with less stress, you grow in confidence and mature in self-perception.

1

Outcome Thinking™: How Did It Start?

What you are about to learn took almost twenty years to pull into one clear thought pattern. After that, it took years of practice to develop my new way of thinking.

Two key lessons I learned helped change how I communicate with others and from these lessons Outcome Thinking™ was born.

Going Back In Time…

First Lesson:

Even though I was too young, I really wanted to swim with the big kids in the deep end of the pool. The shallow end was boring to me. So, even though it was off limits for me, I really wanted to go down the big slide in the deep end. I waited until Mom was distracted by my older brothers and sisters and Dad was on the high dive.

I scrambled up the slide victorious! I realized one slight problem as I slid down…I didn't know how to swim.

I went under three times before my Dad was able to get to me. Petrified, I clung to Dad and begged him to take me out of the water. But he wouldn't. Instead he made me stay in the water and learn to bob. He said I couldn't let the water get the best of me. That if I really wanted to go down the slide then I needed to learn to swim. And then he made me go down the slide again and again until I could swim alone.

He focused on the outcome I wanted and helped me develop the skills to make it happen. He didn't let me cop out or be coddled when I went under. He just made me realize that I was accountable for learning the skills necessary to achieve the outcome I desired.

> *Lesson Learned: For everything you want in life, you need to be willing to hold yourself accountable to learn the skills to make it happen.*

Second Lesson:

My sister and I fought like cats and dogs. We were intense to put it mildly. One day we got sick of the fighting. We decided that before we could snap a quick retort to each other we had to follow some new ground rules. We had to say what we heard the other person say, let the other person say if that is what they meant and then we could respond.

Well, a funny thing happened. We virtually quit fighting. We realized that most of our fights were about us misinterpreting what the other person meant!

> *Lesson Learned: When communicating, most anger and frustration come from misinterpreting what the other person said. Misinterpretation comes from clinging to what we would mean if we had said what the other person said!*

Sound Good? Read On...

This got me thinking how most conflicts and frustrations come from people responding solely from their own point of view, and assuming the other person meant something that might not even be true, much less relevant.

This marinated in my subconscious for two decades before I took it out again and really began to consider how I could use this as an adult. I took this way of thinking and started applying it to training, managing, selling, negotiating and relating to others. What I found was that I wasn't stressed any more! I realized I did not have to state my opinions so strongly to be seen as strong. For me, that was nothing short of miraculous.

Most of all I learned that for all I knew, I knew very little about other people. It was pretty humbling going from having all the answers to viewing myself as a sponge learning from others, but boy was it rewarding.

If you have a strong personality like mine, you might find that changing your communicating style is difficult at times. At first, you might feel like you are giving in. Nothing could be further from the truth! In reality you are leaving yourself open to more possibilities and being more creative which empowers you.

There's Got To Be A Better Way...

This new communication skill is Outcome Thinking™. With it you will be able to have smoother personal relationships, calm family discussions, and creative negotiations.

Imagine having the key to solve these everyday frustrations:

- You are waiting for a friend at a restaurant. Once again he is late and as you wait you get more and more irritated. You hate waiting, but you don't want to damage the relationship by telling him.

- Your boss drops off yet another project and gives only vague direction on what has to be done. You are knee-deep in her other projects. You get annoyed that she has no consideration for you and is so haphazard with projects. Still, she's your boss, so you stay silent.

- Your cube mate at work loves to chat incessantly. You can't concentrate on work when she talks, so you have to stay late to catch up. On top of that, she always leaves precisely at 5:00 p.m., whether or not all the work is done. You want to keep a good working relationship, so you simply hope things change.

Such irritating events happen every day. Wouldn't you love to be able to connect better with others? To be able to be more persuasive without being pushy?

Typically, we spend most of our energy trying to figure out how we can make the other person understand our position or we clam up and suffer in silence. This way of thinking leads to arguments or festering ill will. As the saying goes, "If you do what you've always done, you'll get what you've always gotten." Maybe it's time to stop thinking about *Process* and start thinking about *Outcome*.

This book will show you a whole new way to communicate, a way to reduce stress, eliminate assumptions, and reduce tension under difficult situations. You will learn how to see things from the other person's perspective and focus on the results you want rather than on the process of how to get there. You will learn to listen in a whole new way that draws in, not only what the other person is saying, but what they are trying to say.

It will help you let go of some of the things that keep us stuck in our communication. When you apply this new way of thinking you will find that your stress goes down and you connect better with others. And you will find it doesn't mean drastically altering your personality and it doesn't mean memorizing a lot of phrases.

It does mean locking into a new way of thinking. I am going to share with you the three communication stoppers, why we fall into them and how to break them. These three little things cause the most misinterpretation, hurt feelings and assumptions. They are what drives wedges in families and keep companies in chaos. They are what keep you in a "Me" communication style.

I will share with you the three principles of Outcome Thinking™ and how they shatter the three communication stoppers. I will show you how to apply these every day in every conversation. These three little principles can be the difference between you finding the love you want, the job you desire and the pay you deserve. These three little principles will bring you towards others, as you understand yourself better. Your energy will begin to radiate out and be a magnet for others.

But don't take my word for it. I want you to experience your own journey. One person I coached used this to get a $30,000 raise, another person used it to negotiate from a 7% raise to a 21% raise, another person used it to get promoted two levels. One manager used it to pull his team together and to become a stronger leader.

How You May Benefit From This Book

- If you are in sales and hate pushy sales techniques, this book will give you simple new ways to connect with customers. Your customers will see you as a partner and will welcome your ideas and input.

- If you are a shy person, this book will give you new confidence with people. Even the most introverted can use Outcome Thinking™ to connect with others and be assertive without feeling guilty.

- If you are aspiring to become a manager or simply desire to be a better leader, this book offers key techniques that will help you understand what makes people tick so you can focus on being a stronger team player.

- If you are seeking a more calm and rewarding life, Outcome Thinking™ will help you keep balance and focus in your life. Imagine the benefits of knowing how to keep things in their proper perspective!

- If you're in customer service, you will learn how to make customers comfortable so they want to do business with you. You will learn how to use these skills so that, even if you have to say "no", your customer will still feel valued and recognize that you did the best you could.

Whether you are a CEO, a college student, a high school drop out or a broom pusher, I believe this can help you find the love you want, the job you desire, and the pay you deserve. It will require some work but I know you can do it. Once you start using this new way of communicating you will find that negotiations, handling difficult situations and standing up for yourself can all be done without sweat. And yes, they can even be positive experiences.

As you read this book, write down how you will apply the techniques to interact better with your family, your spouse, your employees, your co-workers, and your friends.

I hope this book gives you as much contentment and peace of mind to read as it gave me to write.

I am excited to be a part of your journey!

PART ONE

What is Outcome Thinking™?

Outcome Thinking™: The Three Principles

What is Outcome Thinking™ And How Does It Work?

Definition: *Outcome Thinking™ is the ability to focus on an outcome desired and then speak from the other person's perspective on how and why to reach that outcome. It is a way of thinking that produces a new result with how others see you, hear you and connect with you. The most ironic part is that it focuses less on you yet it draws people more to you.*

This chapter will explore how Outcome Thinking™ differs from most communication. You will learn the three communication stoppers that keep most of us communicating in a "ME" communication style. You will then learn the three key principles and how they shatter each of the communication stoppers. These three principles are the key elements to success with Outcome Thinking™.

Driving Outcome Thinking™:
It's More Than Just Putting The Gas In!

I want you to imagine you are just learning to drive a car. Remember all those hours in drivers education where they told you what to do and how to do it? Remember how you couldn't wait to get at the wheel because you were sure you had all the answers? And then you got on the road. And it was hard to remember to watch for one way roads, merging traffic or other unforeseen obstacles. And the first time you hit a patch of dry ice and skidded, you wished you had paid more attention in class. And you realized you may have needed some more information or practice.

Learning Outcome Thinking™ will be a bit like driving a car. You see this first chapter will give you the overview. And you may want to run out and just apply what you learned immediately. You'll think "I've got it! I want to use this right away." And you may crash and burn. Just like driving the car before you have really tested out the car's reaction to your foot on the gas pedal and your hands on the steering wheel.

How To Read This Book
·····························

So here is how you want to go through this: First read this chapter and see it as an overview (like drivers education), then read the next four chapters and see them as preparing and conditioning you to be in prime Outcome Thinking™ mode (like learning how the car actually runs versus just learning where to put the gas in) and see the last part as showing you exactly how smoothly Outcome Thinking™ works when it is all put together (like the difference between a well tuned car and one that has major problems waiting to happen).

A Key Belief You Need To Embrace...
···

Outcome Thinking™ makes one key assumption that all points pivot on. If you don't believe this one core thing then I can tell you Outcome Thinking™ will not work for you. You need to wrap your arms around this one belief because it will affect your thoughts and your body language; all of which need to be in agreement when you use Outcome Thinking™

You need to believe that people do things with the best intentions.

If you see people as manipulative, conniving or devious, you will always be trying to read negative things into what they say. You will feel that others are out to get you and that you need to get them first. If you think that way, then you will most likely read this book and feel it is a way to manipulate and control others and you will miss the essence of this book. **I do not want you to use this to control another person**. I do want you to use this to gain control over yourself, to believe in yourself and then to believe the best in others.

Please keep this thought always in your mind as you apply Outcome Thinking™:

People will try to live up to my expectation of them. If I believe the best in others, then I will most likely draw out the best in others. If I believe the worst in others, then I will most likely drive people to be more negative and controlling. By believing the best in myself and others, then I will be helping my thoughts and body language to be open and positive when talking with others. For my body language is tied to my thoughts and tells people how to interpret what I just said. So it must be positive.

Starting With What Keeps You In A "ME" Communication

So let's start with what keeps us communicating from a "ME" perspective. Let's face it, we all want to connect better with others and we certainly do not want to intentionally add stress to our lives. But we do. We spend so much of our communication energy on trying to get people to see what we mean, why we mean it and what we want them to do about it. We want to pull that other person to our perspective—the "ME" perspective. Of course, we assume they will see the light and agree with us. Wrong! Usually it just ticks people off and they spend all their time trying to get you to understand their perspective. And the vicious cycle begins.

In order to best see what the "ME" perspective is and then how we can break it, we need to examine the three communication stoppers that keeps us in a "ME" communication style. These three communication stoppers are very powerful and each one plays off of the other. They aren't easy to break but they all can be overcome with practice.

The First Communication Stopper

The Judgment Factor: I Know Exactly What You Meant!

Here we listen to what a person says and we filter it through the following three thoughts:
   ◆ What do I think of you?
   ◆ What do I think you think of me?

◆ How do I view me?

These three thoughts can cause us to completely misinterpret what a person said. They can cause a "spin on words."

Here we look to have our thoughts, ideas and ourselves validated by other people. We think "if people agree with me and view me positively then that must be the true me." This can lead to us constantly trying to please others. It can frustrate us and it can cause a lot of misinterpretation and assumptions.

Here's How The Judgment Factor Works...

Jane and Tom meet a new consultant Joe. Jane finds Joe egotistical, arrogant and condescending. Tom finds Joe confident, smooth and knowledgeable.

Joe sees Tom handle a difficult client. Joe later approaches Tom and says "That was wonderful how you handled that customer. I was really impressed." Tom will most likely say thanks and ask Joe what he specifically liked about the interaction. Tom will feel very good about the feedback.

Now let's say Joe sees Jane handle a difficult client and he approaches her and says, "That was wonderful how you handled that customer. I was really impressed." (Same words and body language as he used with Tom.) Jane probably thinks "who made you the judge of what I do? It is just one more way for you to feel superior."

What's The Difference?

The only difference between the two interpretations is the filter they each used to hear the message. Tom filtered his through "Joe is a good guy that respects me" and Jane filtered hers through "Joe is an egotistical guy that thinks he is better than me." This difference in thought caused them each to put their own "spin" on Joe's words.

The judgment factor by itself can keep us spinning in a negative tone when we talk with others or listen to others. Now when you layer on the next communication stopper it pushes you deeper in to "ME" communication.

The Second Communication Stopper

Paradigms: Perception Becomes Reality

Paradigms are the way we see and view things. They are rooted in our own experiences or are things we have learned intellectually that we hold on to and believe. They are formed by the way we are raised, the country we are raised in, the religion we are raised with, as well as the environment around us.

We then take all of these experiences and learning, form them in to paradigms that we use as the outside boundaries of the box we think within. They help you decipher what is right or wrong. They are often your compass that tells you how to react to things such as change.

The problem comes not in having paradigms, but in having them so rigidly drawn that we can't flex to see things another way. We believe everyone should have our same value or belief system and we judge others when they do not have our same belief system.

We start saying, "because it's always that way," "we tried that it didn't work," or "he'll never change." We become rigid in how we view things.

You need to be able to see paradigms as guidelines rather than hard cold facts. And you need to decipher the importance of them and the flexibility you want with them. Some paradigms, such as your religious beliefs, help you stay in line with what is morally right or wrong. Here you might say "I won't change my beliefs but I also won't impose them on others." Other paradigms you may need to let go of or redefine.

Imagine that you grew up believing that, with the exception of some finger foods, all food should be eaten with the fork in the right hand. This is the way you were raised, your paradigm. Then you travel to a foreign country where everyone eats with their hands. If you are rigid with your paradigm you may think they are all heathens because they don't eat with utensils. If you instead realize that it's just different from you, you may just decide you prefer to eat with utensils and you don't think poorly of anyone in that country that eats with their hands. You don't judge them by your paradigm. But you also don't try to convert them to your paradigm. They do not validate your choice of eating with utensils or your hands. It is just a preference.

Paradigms can push us strongly into the third communication stopper because we try to justify our paradigms with right and wrong thinking.

The Third Communication Stopper

Right And Wrong Thinking

Right and wrong thinking means you want to know who is right and who is wrong. Or what is right and what is wrong. You feel a need to justify your answer. You look for others to validate who you are and what you feel or think. This third communication stopper works closely with the "judgment factor" and can keep us from truly hearing the other person's message.

Right And Wrong Thinking In Action...

Here is a typical example of right and wrong thinking: Jane asks Tom to fax her a proposal for her 2 p.m. meeting the next day. Tom says he will. At noon the next day Jane still does not have the fax.

With right and wrong thinking Jane starts to fume. "Didn't I say I needed this for a 2 p.m. meeting? He always does things at the last minute. I can't believe he blew me off like this. Now I have to waste my time tracking him down to get this." She feels disgust and anger. In her mind, he's wrong, she's right.

You see, **right and wrong thinking requires laying blame on someone.** Instead of focusing on the outcome desired—Jane needed the paper for her meeting—she instead involves all her emotion and energy on who is right and who is wrong.

Have you ever done this?

In fact, if Jane were honest with herself, there's plenty of blame to go around. She admits she *knows* Tom always waits until the last minute, yet she gave him a vague, open-ended request for the report. The only time she mentioned was 2 p.m. By Tom's standards, 1:55 p.m. is "before" 2:00 p.m. If Jane wanted the report by noon, she should have said noon.

The Bigger Point Is...

But the bigger point is ...

◆ Why does there need to be an absolute right and wrong?

◆ Why do we need to prove ourselves to others?

◆ How can we step away from these three communication stoppers, especially since they are so easily fed upon by each other? They can be a vicious cycle that keep us wallowing in negative "ME" communication.

These are all great questions and are what led me to Outcome Thinking™. Each principle of Outcome Thinking™ shatters one of the communication stoppers. Let's examine each of the principles and what communication stopper it shatters. Let's begin with the key ingredient.

Change Your Thinking With Three Easy Principles

The First Key Principle Of Outcome Thinking™: Find The Value

Start by thinking, **"How can I add value to this person?"** Every time you communicate this needs to be foremost in your mind. Your energy has to be on the other person first, not on yourself.

What do I mean by "adding value"? Well, simply stated, "adding value" means showing respect. You care enough about each individual's worth to deliberately seek out the positive and focus on that. You make them feel good! You expect and believe the best in others. You draw out the best in them.

There are two reasons this step is so important. One, it trains you to phrase your thoughts in a positive manner. Whether you are negotiating, networking, talking with a co-worker, or speaking with your spouse, you will always be thinking of positive things to say and the most effective ways to phrase those thoughts. *Yes, you can train your subconscious mind to automatically search for the good in a situation.* Even difficult situations become easier when you are able to make the other person feel good.

Respect Before You Expect

Remember, people will try to live up to the expectation they believe you have of them. The more straightforward you are with your information, the more you show the person that you believe in them and their abilities, the better they will react to you and what you say.

Secondly, it frees you from the mistaken assumption we tend to make when we communicate—that what others think or do validates or discredits us personally. We all worry about how people are going to perceive what we say, so we too often sacrifice candor and clarity in an effort to get them to validate what *we* feel. Therefore, we tend to phrase things in ways designed to elicit approval from others, rather than to truly communicate. When you focus on adding value to others, people will want to be around you and to hear what you have to say.

Shatter The Judgment Factor

You are able to shatter the "judgment factor" because you don't worry about how other people view you. You assume they see the best in you like you see the best in others. You listen to what they say as though that is exactly what they meant to say. You don't try to read anything deeper into their message. And if you are confused you ask for clarity because you assume you must not be hearing their message correctly, not that they are trying to "pull one over" on you.

Do you notice the major shift here? Instead of communicating and thinking from a "ME" perspective, you start communicating from a "WE" perspective. You remove the focus from *you* and instead focus on making the other person comfortable. In doing so, the happy and almost effortless result is that you too will be more comfortable.

Once you have applied this then you wrap all of your conversations in focusing on the outcome desired which leads us to our next key principle.

Focus On The Outcome Desired, Not The Process Of How To Get There.

The Second Key Principle Of Outcome Thinking™

Now that you have applied the first principle and you are focusing on the other person, you need to find an easy way to stop the other person from focusing on the emotional side of communication. Remember even though you are using Outcome Thinking™, the other party is probably still in the "ME" communication mode. So we need to have Outcome Thinking™ have a way to pull all parties to a nonjudgmental way of communicating.

You do this by focusing on the outcome desired. Ask yourself, "What is my bottom-line need for this situation?" What is the result you want? Why would they want this result? Focusing on the outcome keeps you from holding on to how things were done or are currently being done.

Shatters Rigid Paradigms

It frees up your creativity and it shatters our second communication stopper- rigid paradigms. It allows people to safely let go of how they thought things should be and opens their subconscious mind to finding ways to make the outcome happen. It breaks what I call "process thinking."

Of course, I don't mean that you should ignore processes. Processes are essential tools we use to get a result, but they are not the end product. Like "company policy" or "standard operating procedures," our communication processes must be discarded when they no longer serve their intended purpose. They must not be something we cling to. Processes will change over time. They are meant to assist communication, not to define communication. Outcome is the "why" you want the result or the "what" you'll benefit from the result while the process is the "how" you'll get the result.

Don't Get Derailed

Let's say you want to negotiate a raise. If you follow the normal process, you will probably wait until review time, see what the company gives you and then go back to negotiate why you need a raise. That is the standard process.

Now try it this way: focus on the result you want. "I want to raise my standard of living." Now you look at educational opportunities, car allowances, days off, commission, raise, etc. You don't limit yourself.

You would approach management when you feel it is appropriate rather than being constrained by the dictates of review time. The raise itself is not a "result" it is a process. Money has no inherent value other than as a tool of exchange for the results you really want. By the way, it is *easier* to get a raise when they are considering only you, not when they are doling out raises to everyone!

Keep Your Eye On The Prize

Remember, processes are good when they provide guidelines for what we are doing; they help streamline how we work. They are counterproductive when they restrict our options, dictating what we can and can't do. Processes should be designed to aid us in getting to the result, not to inhibit us.

Do you have any processes that you need to get rid of? What are you doing right now because it has "always been done that way"? Challenge yourself to see things from a fresh perspective!

Think And Speak Positively
From The Other Person's Perspective
The Third Key Principle Of Outcome Thinking™

Travel Light And You'll Go
Farther Faster—Dump The Baggage!

Remember our third communication stopper? That good old right and wrong thinking. Well we need a way to break that thought pattern. We need to be able to understand that we can't always be right and that often there is more than one right answer. So we need a way to open ourselves up to more ways of thinking and seeing things.

Shatter Right And Wrong Thinking!

You do that by thinking and speaking from the other person's perspective. This thought pattern helps you let go of pettiness, defenses, assumptions and narrow perceptions. It means acknowledging that you might not be right. It allows you to be open to the other person, to truly listen and to remove defenses. This is NOT an easy step. Once you master this, you will find that people are more interesting and can teach you a great deal. We are truly all different, and you will learn to treasure and benefit from these differences.

TAKE ACTION

Put your hands around your right eye, cupping them like a telescope. Now close your left eye and look through your telescope. What do you see? Focus on an object in the room. How much space does it now take up in your telescope?

This illustrates the narrow viewpoint we bring to our communications when we limit ourselves to one perspective. Now remove your hands and look around the room with both eyes. Wow! See how much you missed?

The "whole room" viewpoint is what we get when we look at things from the other person's perspective. The object that consumed most of the field in your telescope, no longer dominates the entire picture. By considering other's points of view we see things in relation to the big picture.

If we don't speak and see things from the other person's perspective we can end up putting too much emphasis on things that really don't have any relevance to the outcome we desire. When you are communicating with others, remind yourself to keep your telescope tucked away.

In order to best use this third step you might need to role-play with others for you might not be able to see where the other person is coming from until someone else points it out. The key thing is to realize that you might not see things eye to eye and that is okay. No one person needs to be right all the time. And being wrong doesn't mean we are weak. Actually most of your strength comes from just believing in yourself, validating yourself and not looking for others to validate you.

Here's how it looks....

THREE COMMUNICATION STOPPERS	SHATTERED BY USING THIS PRINCIPLE →	**THREE KEY PRINCIPLES**

1. The Judgment Factor.

You interpret what you think the other person means by looking at how you perceive them and how you believe they perceive you. This causes you to read in to what they said. Cycles back and forth with right and wrong thinking.

 SHATTERED BY →

1. How can I "add value" to this person?

What you say should build a person's self-esteem and show you have belief in their integrity and desire to do the right thing.

"Believes the best in others"

2. Rigid Paradigms.

Paradigms cause you to look at things one way and block your creativity. Comes from way we were raised, environment we were raised in. Shapes our values.

 SHATTERED BY →

2. Focus on the outcome you desire, not the process of how to get there.

Being results oriented causes you to find new ways to do things. Make sure you are focused on the deepest outcome desired. Allows others to own and participate in the process.

3. Right and Wrong Thinking.

We worry about who is right and who is wrong. This causes you to look for why they did what they did and justify why you did what you did.

 SHATTERED BY →

3. Think and speak POSITIVELY from the other person's perspective.

What are their challenges? How might they be feeling or thinking? What do they have to gain or lose in this situation? How can you appeal to their desires?

ME COMMUNICATION	**VS**	**WE COMMUNICATION**

These Three Steps Shift You In
Three Key Ways When You Communicate

One, because you add value to each person, you no longer worry about whether people like you or what they think about you. You automatically assume people do like you and therefore, you take all communication at face value without looking for hidden meanings.

Two, you no longer focus on you. Instead you focus on the other person and put things in perspective. You start to see the big picture.

Three, you move from thinking "right versus wrong" to more productive thought, thinking how to reach the outcome desired. You don't waste time and energy with worry about justifying things or defending things; you look for solutions.

So How Does This Translate To Me?

So how can you use this skill in your own life? How can you connect better with others? In order to be able to apply these skills you need to review four key areas of your own life. These four areas will make or break how you apply the three key principles. They cannot be ignored or you may incorrectly apply the principles you just learned. Think of these four areas as learning all the intricate details of how the car works. If you ignore one, you may end up with just a pile of junk that used to get you around.

To best understand why these four areas are so important I want to illustrate how they can affect how you communicate.

Going Deeper....
Below the surface of:

THREE COMMUNICATION STOPPERS	AND	THREE KEY PRINCIPLES

Negative tone. Assumes people are trying to manipulate you. Keeps you in "Judgment Factor"

← YOUR SELF-TALK →

Positive tone. Assumes the best in you. Helps you "add value" to others.

Think you have to out think others. Believe there is little you have done that is great. Keeps you in Right and Wrong thinking.

← YOUR THOUGHT → PROCESS

Positive. Believe in yourself. Look to focus on what you can affect. Focus on your successes and strengths. Helps you see things from the other person's perspective.

Look for others to validate you. Scared to face change. Keeps you in Right and Wrong thinking.

← YOUR MENTAL → PICTURE

Positive. See yourself as constantly evolving and learning. Gives you strength to validate yourself. Helps with seeing things from the other person's perspective.

See as rigid. "Box you live in"

← YOUR → PARADIGMS

See as guidelines. See self as a "learning sponge."

ME COMMUNICATION	VS	WE COMMUNICATION

You can see how each one of these becomes critical to how you either stay stuck in the Communication Stoppers or shatter them and apply Outcome Thinking™. The next part of this book will take you through these key areas, how they affect how you communicate and how to reroute them so you can use Outcome Thinking™.

So Here's The Plan...

I encourage you to write notes in the margins and use a high-lighter as you go through this book. It's also very helpful to keep a journal. When you get to the real life examples, don't feel com-pelled to read through in the order they're presented. Instead, go to the area that applies to you. Remember, the sections are broken down with examples to include working with your co-workers, your boss, your customers, your employees and your family and friends. Jump around and read the ones that interest you the most. Take some of the examples and try to work through them. You're going to be working on shifting your energies to *results,* not processes, so you can start right now by using this book in the way you will get the quickest results.

A Caveat And An Invitation

Don't read the real life examples as gospel. They are merely examples of how to use a new way of thinking to handle difficult situations. I don't want you to try memorizing them, instead just try to capture the thought process. I included them because a lot of books tell you about a skill but don't show you how to apply it. I wanted this book to be practical and immediately applicable. You might even choose to read the examples first! Remember, taking whatever works best for you and the results you want is part of your new way of thinking!

Let's begin your journey...

PART TWO

Developing
the Skills

C H A P T E R   T W O

Self-Talk

Do You Hear Voices? You'd Be Crazy Not To!

Do you talk to yourself? You are probably asking yourself, "Do I talk to myself. I'm not sure?" We all talk to ourselves with what is called our critical voice. Per Julie White, a psychologist, we develop this voice at age 4!! Of course, it is usually not a very sophisticated voice! The good news is that you can effectively change your critical voice, but first let's look at how it works.

Critical Voice

Your critical voice is both positive and negative. It's the voice that tells you that you're doing a great job, and the voice that tells you that you're pathetic. It is the voice you use to review your performance in all situations. Your critical voice is rooted in your subconscious mind. Just becoming aware that you use this voice is the first step.

Recognizing Your Own Voice: Look Who's Talking!

There are several different aspects to your critical voice and you may alternate or use a combination of them. To better understand all of your voices let's walk through an example of locking your keys in your car. Per Julie White, here is how each voice might typically respond:

> *Rambo:* "How could you possibly lock the keys in the car. You're so stupid. How could you miss taking the keys out of the ignition? You'd forget your head if it weren't attached." (gets angry with you)

27

Teacher: "Well, what can you learn from this? Maybe you need a big bright key chain or a car that only locks with the key." (looks to learn)

Parent: "Well, what are you going to do now?" (places blame)

Mr. Rogers/Pollyanna: "This is great. I'll get to meet a new police officer." (looks for the silver lining)

Friend: "Don't worry about it. You look great today." (looks to excuse you)

Which Voice Do You Use?

You might use a series of voices. Each of them has good and bad points. The Friend voice, if used with the Teacher voice, is a good combination. It's productive and builds your self-esteem. The Friend voice used by itself can let you off the hook too easily and never hold you accountable for your own actions. The Parent voice used alone is often harsh; doesn't give you a break. It is ready to point out what you did wrong and not let you wiggle out of it. The Parent voice does, however, make your subconscious mind search for an answer. Holding yourself accountable is a positive aspect.

Don't Use That Tone Of Voice With Me!

The one voice you absolutely do not need is the Rambo voice. This voice attacks you personally and *does* damage your *self-perception*. In order to change this voice you first need to become aware of the voice. When you hear it, say "Stop or Cancel." I mean this literally! If you're alone, say it out loud. If you're with others, say it silently to yourself. The important thing is to break the negative thought pattern. Then replace that attack with a positive statement.

The easiest and most rewarding voice is the Teacher. It is always accepting of you and tries to get you to search for reasons or answers that are within your control. It assumes there is a possible solution, and that you are capable of discovering it. The Teacher voice often triggers your subconscious mind to work beyond its present capacity. When using this voice, new ideas and paradigm shifts occur.

We use our various voices on others as well as ourselves; situations are interpreted through this filter. We can ascribe differing motives and intents to others based upon which voice is interpreting.

TAKE ACTION: WORK ON YOUR VOICE!

The best place to work on creating a new voice is in your car. As you drive around try responding to situations with various voices. For example, when a car changes into your lane and almost cuts you off, the Rambo voice might respond with anger. "What a jerk! Is he blind?" The Parent voice might say, "That guy is the perfect argument for driver tests to renew a license." The Teacher might say, "Boy that was a close call. Maybe I should hang back a little." The Pollyanna/Mr. Rogers voice might say, "He must be in a hurry. I sure hope he gets where he's going in time." And the Friend voice takes your side: "How rude. I can't believe he didn't even look for me." See how each voice influences our response?

You want to train yourself to see things from all perspectives. Assume the best of the other person. Maybe the other person is feeling rather foolish for cutting you off or honestly did not see you. Perhaps you weren't as attentive as you should have been. Regardless, this is a good exercise for learning to recognize various perspectives.

Thoughts Have Power
·························

You will find that, as you take yourself through these different thoughts, a variety of emotions will run through your head. (Thoughts trigger emotions and our thoughts come from our critical voice.) Have you ever met someone that you thought was nice, but not exceptional? And then later on you hear that they thought you were wonderful and now your regard for them jumps up ten notches! What changed? The only thing that changed was your perspective once you received new information.

When you first start becoming aware of your critical voice it may feel awkward. You may feel odd talking to yourself—especially out loud. Keep in mind that it is perfectly normal! After all, you have spent a lifetime developing your habits; you can't reverse them overnight. The more control you gain over your Self-Talk the more control and positive energy you will notice in your life.

Self-Talk Is Self-Fulfilling

Amazingly, our Self-Talk affects us physically as well as mentally.

TAKE ACTION

Try this experiment. Have someone stand with her right arm extended parallel to the ground, her hand in a fist. Place both of your hands on her arm, and try to push it back down to her side. (It will resemble pumping for water on an old water pump handle.) Then tell the person to say out loud ten times, "I am a weak person." She will then put the same arm up again in the same position for you to push down. See how easy it is this time?

Even though the person may not truly believe that they are weak, the Self-Talk sends messages to the muscles telling them to respond weakly. Such a powerful force should be harnessed for positive results, not left to the whim of our changing moods.

Self-Talk And Your Self-Image

Mirror, Mirror On The Wall…

Do other people's words affect your self-image? The surprising answer is NO. What you say to *yourself* after the other person stops talking is what affects you.

Let's say I make the following three comments to different people. 1) "You are very unorganized," 2) "You are very nice looking," 3) "You have nice purple hair." The purple hair comment is demonstrably false. You can look in the mirror, see you don't have purple hair, and dismiss the comment. The first two statements are more subjective and therefore need to be interpreted through your critical voice. Both comments—"You are unorganized," and "You are very attractive."—can be taken positively and will boost your self-image. Or, they can be taken negatively and damage your self-image.

Who You Gonna Believe?

The positive critical voice will respond to the unorganized comment by thinking, "I am actually very organized in my own way and am able to get my hands on everything I need." The positive critical voice responds to the pretty comment with a "Thank you." The negative critical voice will respond to the comments with "My gosh this person just met me and she can already see how unorganized I am. I must be really bad," or, "Me? Attractive? Oh, not really. I have zits, and a gap in my front tooth."

Quit Talking Yourself Out Of Compliments

Oddly, it's common to use the negative critical voice when responding to compliments from others. Why? Because we are taught not to brag and that others won't want to be around us if we do. This conditioning surfaces inappropriately when we are trying to accept a compliment. Often we will respond by pointing out the negative: "It is really old." "I just threw it together. Really it was nothing." "Anyone could have done it." "It was really cheap." Next time you are handed a compliment try just saying, "Thank you!"

Self-Talk And Stress

The real kicker is that 70% of our Self-Talk is stress producing!!! Think about it! 70% of our stress could be self-induced. Wow! Rather than interpreting this as an indictment of our own behavior, we should be cheering—we now know that we have the *power* to reduce stress, rather than being helpless victims. The more you work at controlling your critical voice to keep it positive, the less stress you will have in your life.

If You're In No Mood To Listen To Yourself, Who Else Is?

The next time you find yourself in a stressful situation try talking yourself through it in a positive manner. Let's say that your workload has gotten increasingly heavy, (not hard to imagine!). Instead of stressing out about it, take a deep breath and say, "I can positively impact these projects." Then physically remove yourself from the stressful place—another room, outside—and sit down with a piece of paper and think it through. List each project and ask yourself, "What's the worst thing that can happen if this does not get done?" This will help you prioritize your tasks in order of importance. Work on the projects that help with the long term, delegate where you can and let go of perfectionism.

Ask Yourself Questions—Listen To The Answer—Then Share The News!

I have seen people use this system to eliminate a lot of stress in their lives, largely by eliminating unnecessary projects. One man realized that three weekly projects that took up 30% of his time seemed to have little importance. He brought this to the attention of his boss and they eliminated those three projects!

I use this system to organize my office. If I notice that I am feeling stressed, I ask myself, "What things am I doing over and over again?" Then I create a one-time formula for that project to knock out the repetition. This way of thinking has helped me triple my business, reduce my hours at work, while at the same time increasing my ability to customize for my clients. All of that without any additional staff. It's like discovering a new source of time and energy!

Self-Talk And Your Subconscious

Pssst....This Is Your Subconscious Speaking...

You will find times in your life where having a neat little system just doesn't seem to work, times when your critical voice really hammers down on you. You beat yourself up. Sound familiar?

What do you do when you know your boss does not think you are doing a good job? When you know your in-laws don't like you?

At these times your control over your critical voice is more important than ever.

Turning Negatives Into Positives

Only Kodak Needs Negatives—Be Positive!

When you are facing a tough meeting, negotiation, interview or situation, you absolutely have to repeat positive thoughts to yourself. Remember, your mind believes what it hears. It trusts you implicitly, and will eagerly coordinate your speech and actions to match what you think. Matter of fact, your thoughts will always show in your body language. So if you tell yourself you are defeated, that no one will support your idea, or that your boss doesn't like you, your body language will match those thoughts. You might sit in a slouched position, break eye contact too often, shuffle your fingers and succumb to any nervous tics you have. (You must control your thoughts in order to control your body language.) In later chapters we will look at our body language and its relationship to your thoughts.

Changing Your Critical Voice And Self-Talk

If Your Negative Voice Calls, Hang Up

You may be thinking, this is all nice, but *how* do I change my critical voice? The first step is being aware of what your critical voice is saying. Most of the time we're unaware of our Self-Talk. Start truly listening to yourself. What is your voice saying to you? When you catch yourself in a negative statement say, "Stop, Stop" or "Cancel, Cancel." However you wish to say it, you must change the statement right then and there. Replace it with a positive statement. Your subconscious mind will believe what you say.

> **TAKE ACTION**
>
> Ask yourself, "What did my voice say to me today?"
> What did you say when you woke up this morning? What
> were your thoughts as you got ready to go out the door
> today? Did your day match what your thoughts were?

Case History: Me.

The other day I flew to Chicago for a speaking engagement. I left in the morning in a good mood, but I had a nagging doubt that something would go wrong. When I got to the airport, I found they had oversold the plane and storage space was limited. I'd planned ahead, bringing a bag that fit in the overhead bins so I wouldn't run the risk of losing it. You guessed it—they made me check the bag at the gate.

To be on the safe side, I unlocked my suitcase and took out the essential materials for my speech, and put them in my briefcase, along with a small canvas bag. As I took out the canvas bag, I kept thinking, "You're going to lose this." When the flight landed, I retrieved my suitcase and realized I had lost my keys to unlock it! Since I was in a time crunch I had to run and catch a ride to my hotel. Throughout all of this, I tried to find the humor in it, but also kept telling myself, "I knew something like this would happen."

Then, when I arrived at the hotel I realized that I no longer had the canvas bag!! Since I had been telling myself that I would lose it, my subconscious mind was happy to make that happen.

A Tale Of Premonition: I Told Myself This Would Happen!

On the positive side, I have also had many nights where I have gone to bed and prayed that tomorrow I would have something exciting happen or that I would close a new deal. Every time I have done this, I have closed a new deal the next day! I recently told my husband about this, commenting how eerie it was. I asked him what he thought it meant. "I don't know," he said with a mischievous laugh, " but why don't you do it more often!"

Listen To The Voice Of Reason

If you do nothing else, taking pause to control your thoughts is the single most beneficial thing you can do for yourself and those you love. Think about the messages you send your children. One woman told me how she was standing before the mirror, criticizing her heavy thighs and hips, thinking how ugly she looked. Her five year old daughter looked up at her and said, "Don't say that. I think you're beautiful and I think I am beautiful and if you don't think you're beautiful, does that mean I'm not beautiful either?" What messages we send our children without even realizing it!

I-Witness Reports: Self-Talk
And Your Interpretation Of Events

Have you ever discussed a family event and as you hear the other person relate the story, you think, "Were we at the same event?" Other peoples interpretation of the same event can be so drastically different from yours—not in error, just different. We all process what we hear and see through our own personal experience filter to make a quick interpretation. This is why there can be so many conflicting stories from eyewitnesses. In fact, law enforcement officers are suspicious of eyewitness accounts that match too precisely. It's just not natural. No matter how hard we try to see the truth, we see it from our perspective. We need to pause and try to think from the other person's perspective. By doing so, we do not eliminate our perspective, we add to it and enhance it.

TAKE ACTION

I would like you to write down a mathematical equation that brings you the answer 6. (Uh—uh—uh—Gotcha!) (Don't cheat and read ahead!) Just take the time to write your answer.

Did you write 216 divided by 36? *You didn't?* I did! So, you got the wrong answer! Sound silly? It is.

And yet, we each live our lives as if getting to the answer 6 can only be done *our way*. Once we find the best path *for us*, we spend all our time trying to get other people to take our path. For this validates our choices. In reality there is no better or best, only what works best for us, in getting the desired outcome.

CHAPTER THREE

Thought Process

What Was I Thinking! Let's Think About How You Think

Not only does the way you talk to yourself affect the way you speak to others, so does the way you think. We are trained since birth to focus on the negatives rather than the positives about ourselves. What's the first word a child learns? NO. A research study by the University of Iowa shows that the average two year old hears 432 negative statements and only 32 positive statements in a day! This is what is entering our minds as we learn to talk to ourselves.

Then, we enter school and are taught not to boast or brag. If you accomplish something you learn to say, "It wasn't any big deal." Acknowledging your accomplishments is not only good, it is necessary! Your subconscious mind is nourished by positive input.

The difference between what your subconscious mind believes and what it sees is what motivates you. If you say, "I'm really not a very good artist," your mind tries to make that statement come true. If, however, you say, "I'm not an accomplished artist just yet, but with practice I could be great," you allow your mind to balance the potential and reality. You need to feed your mind with positive statements that your mind wants to make come true.

TAKE ACTION
Success Logs—Write Down The Good Stuff

A good way to develop your skills is to start what I call a "success log." Everyday, write down three successes you had that day. You can even do this at the bottom of your calendar if you wish. Some days you might not have very big successes. For example, some of my days say, "I went to work. I didn't run anyone over and I made it home." And on some days, those are true accomplishments!

We forget or overlook our successes. Don't believe me? Just try to write down twenty successes you have had in your life. Not easy, is it? You should see people's faces when I do this in a seminar. They get blank stares just trying to remember one success! Why? Why is it so hard to see our successes?

We have been trained to look at our failures more than our successes. Think of your work review system. Is it designed to celebrate all the unique things you contribute? Or is it designed to point out solely those things you need to improve on? If reviews really pointed out our good points, wouldn't everyone be excited to get reviewed?

TAKE ACTION

Start now to program your mind for success by remembering all of your successes and celebrating them. Enlist the aid of a "success buddy" and share your successes with each other—no egos involved. It's fun, rewarding, and you will find you will feel more energetic and vibrant.

Curl Up With A Good Book—About You!

TAKE ACTION

Stop here and list some of the successes you have had in your life. Start your success log today. If you work for a corporation this is imperative to your job at review time. The average person reviews herself only based on the last 3 months! That's all you remember. On top of that, most people rely on their manager to remember all the good things they did. If *you* can't remember what you did, how is your manager suppose to remember? Additionally, a supervisor is far more likely to remember negatives than positives.

TAKE ACTION

To combat this, label a file "review" and then stick any complimentary note, recognition or memos you've written about things you have achieved in your job. You will feel great going into your review with all this ammunition. If someone compliments you on a project you did, ask for it in writing to stick in your review folder!

So You Think You're Hot Stuff? Maybe You Are!

Success breeds success. Now I realize that this may feel vain to some of you, especially if you are a shy or reserved person. It still occasionally feels vain to me and I am very outgoing. Plus, it's my own system! But I can tell you that my success log and my "success thinking" have gotten me through many tough times and many tough situations. If you look at it as a tool, rather than an end in itself, you can avoid the feeling that you're being self-absorbed.

Tough Tests For Self-Talk—A Case History

I remember one time in particular that being conscious of my successes really helped me. I was hired by a major real estate chain to speak to each of their offices on how to use impression management to present a better image. I had done eight of the offices and had received rave reviews. However…

One of my upcoming speeches was with an office in an upscale neighborhood. A few days before the program I had a call from Bill, the manager, and we played phone tag. We never did connect. On the day of the program, I arrived and the receptionist ushered me to the meeting room so I could get set up. Once I was ready I went down to talk with Bill. Bill looked at me with horror. "I didn't want you here," he blurted. "You're not set up are you?" Nice greeting, hmm?

Well, you can guess how I felt. He told me his people were "above" such a program and that he would be insulting them to have me speak to them. He finally sighed and agreed to do the program, but said he didn't want to pay for it. Showing him the evaluations from the other offices didn't set him at ease. By this time, I was feeling shattered. I told him that if he felt that way, I would just pack everything up.

Finally he said, "Well, let's just do it, but I'm not pleased with it." Are those words that would inspire you to perform your best? My mind raced with negative self-talk. "You're going to bomb." "There's no way his staff is going to get it if he doesn't support it." "They're going to think what I have to say is beneath them."

Then I stopped myself. I knew those things weren't true. I was a good speaker. I had the write-ups from his other offices to prove it. I started focusing on my past successes. I told myself, "You are going to have a ball today." "They are going to learn so much from you." "They are going to have fun and laugh and learn with you." I kept those thoughts forefront in my mind.

Well, guess what? It was one of my best speeches ever. The best part was the phone calls I got later. Bill was actually referring people to me!

Can You Really Handle This Job? Ask The Expert—You!

That day I learned a big lesson. I had a choice to listen to what Bill had to say and believe it or I could focus on my successes and the outcome I desired. Remember, what the mind believes it can achieve. I would even amend that to "what the mind believes it *will* achieve."

It is not just important to frame your mind with success, it is imperative. So what are those successes? Have you written yours down? (And why haven't you?) Don't feel badly if you can't think of very many yet. Just ask yourself every day, "What were my past successes?" and your mind will eventually bring them up. Be prepared though, because you will usually remember them at the oddest times and never when you have paper! I now keep a tape recorder in my car with me. A child's bathtub crayon would be handy in showers, too!

Thinking Of Improving Your Relationship?

Many of you reading this book are married or involved in a committed relationship. This next part is for you. Your self-talk and your successes affect your relationship. There are no ifs, ands or buts about it. If you are not doing this for work, definitely do it for your relationships. You will be surprised at how much your thought patterns affect the way you view your successes.

My husband and I married at the tender age of twenty-one. We thought we were ready to conquer the world. After seven years of marriage, things fell apart and I asked for a separation. After two years of being apart, some friends told us about Retrouvaille. Retrouvaille is a retreat run by the Catholic Church, but it is non-denominational. It is an intense weekend of counseling that you actually do for yourself.

Well, we had tried the traditional counseling and weren't having any success. Most counselors just pointed out our personality differences and told us we would have to live with them. Frustration was pretty high for us. We just wanted things resolved one way or the other.

So, we decided to try this weekend retreat. At the retreat, no one knew each other's situations, or what you as a couple, needed to work on in your marriage. We were put in a hotel room with no television or radio.

We met as a large group where one couple shared part of their story and we were then given a question to discuss. First, we were separated to write down our answers privately. Then, we got together, read each others answer twice, and explained what we thought we read and responded to it.

Who's The Focus?

Well, after two days of doing this, a revelation hit me. My husband was always writing "we" and I was always writing "I." It dawned on me that maybe the problem with our marriage was the way I looked at marriage. Maybe I was filtering everything through how I thought it affected me rather than looking at how we fit together. That day I started to focus on all the good my husband had to offer.

The funny thing is that once I focused on all the good things he had to offer, it seemed those things happened more often.

TAKE ACTION

Next time you get upset with your spouse stop. Before you give yourself the pleasure of digging into why he/she upset you, list eight things your spouse does that you really like. You will be surprised at how hard it will be to resume thinking about what just annoyed you.

Perception Is Reality

Remember, what you focus on is what you will get back. People try to live up to the perception they believe you have of them. This is why it is so important to tell children what they do really well.

Matter of fact, according to a Harvard study, what you say during the day replays on average three to four times in your mind, but what you say at night replays nine to eleven times. So when you tuck your children in at night, tell them what you think they did really well that day and ask them what they felt good about. For yourself, it is imperative that you go to bed replaying the good things you did that day and also listing what great things you will accomplish tomorrow.

Isn't the power of the mind amazing? I am always fascinated by people who want to gain control over their lives, but they don't want to try to control their thoughts. Your thoughts are the beginning of the journey. Be always conscious of them and make sure you make them positive!!

Nourish Your Family With More Than Food

TAKE ACTION

I recommend that one day a week you have a dinner conversation as a family that centers around your successes that week. Each person gets to relate something they did well. Be sure to give everyone equal time and parents, be sure you tell your successes as well. You might want to give this special night its own name to enhance its stature as part of your family tradition. Bring out the good dishes, add some fresh flowers, or have a special dessert—whatever little personal touches you can add will help to make this weekly celebration eagerly anticipated and memorable. Everyone should support and encourage each person. It is important to discuss why it is good to celebrate everyone's success. Remind them to point out friends successes also. This helps your child to keep from boasting and bragging when with friends. This is not only a good family-building activity, it's a great way to learn to think positively.

Reflections Of Yourself

TAKE ACTION

Your successes stay with you for a long time. Take some quiet time to sit back and reflect on your successes from your past. What things have shaped you to be the person you are? Have you ever felt really successful about something you have done and then someone said it wasn't a very big deal? How did you feel? Why do you think someone would try to diminish your success?

If The Silver On Your Mirror Is Tarnished, Borrow A Friend's

Remember that there is only one judge of your success and that is YOU! No one else's opinion matters. All that matters is what you say to yourself about your successes. Sometimes it is hard to find something you feel successful about. At those times, your success buddy is truly your best friend, and will be able to point to all those good things about you that you are unable to see at the moment.

Remember no person is an island unto himself!

Feel The Power

Strengths

UCLA asked incoming freshman to list their strengths and weaknesses. As you know, UCLA is not an easy school to get into, yet every student listed six weaknesses to every one strength! Amazing.

> **TAKE ACTION: Bet You Didn't Know Your Own Strength**
> Take some time right now to list your strengths. The best place to do this is in the first two pages of your success log. I recommend that you add to this list two new strengths every week. By the end of the year you will have 104 strengths about yourself. Quite a list!

Strengths are what get us through our tough times. They push us forward and, in Outcome Thinking™, they provide balance. You need to see your strengths in order to appreciate other people's strengths. In other words, if you can't see your strengths it is difficult for you to give positive power to others.

Positive Power—The Good Stuff
You Have The Power To Be A Hero

Let's explore what I mean by positive power. We all have power. Just like we all have a hero within. Some of us just develop it further than others. Positive Power people want others to learn from their own mistakes, not to repeat them. They praise people and create a team atmosphere. They look for and expect the good in other people. They value what others have to offer.

Positive Power people are strong in their beliefs but don't inflect them on others. They live a life focused on producing positive outcomes with the support of others. Positive Power people realize they are not an island. They share the glory and assume accountability when things go wrong. In a nutshell, they believe they are always evolving, that they are learning sponges and they are not perfect. They give people the benefit of the doubt.

The opposite is negative power. Now negative power would be where you allow others to walk all over you, where you constantly defer to others and where you let someone else have control over your life.

Negative Power—The Bad Stuff

You Have The Power To Be A Doormat

You think: "I'd really like to go to a nice restaurant tonight."
You say: "What would you like to do tonight, honey?"
Spouse says: "A movie sounds good."
You say: "Anything else, maybe?"
Spouse says: "No, just a movie."
You sigh: "Okay," and get ready to go to the movies again.

Secretly you are angry because you feel you always do what your spouse wants instead of what you want. Why should your spouse change if you are always willing to do what they want to do? How assertive are you in asking for what you want? Do you make suggestions and then say, "It's just an idea. What do you think?" Instead start saying, "I really feel like going to a nice restaurant tonight instead of a movie. Is there a particular restaurant you would like to go to? We could take in a late movie then."

You would like to be promoted at work. A great job opens in another department. You talk to your supervisor and ask if she would put in a good word for you. You then sit back to see what happens. You never hear anything about it again. You secretly fume and wonder if your supervisor even put in a good word for you at all.

Who's life is this? Most people relinquish their power to their bosses. Why should your boss be so invested in your career. A better move would be to let your boss know you have liked working for her and that you are ready to be promoted. Mention you saw the opening in the new area and are going to apply for the new position, and would appreciate her assistance. Ask your boss to write a recommendation letter for you. Then approach the manager in the new area and apply for the new job.

Power Struggles With Yourself—Who Wins?

See how simple it can be once we acknowledge that in many instances we are relinquishing our own power? *It's a voluntary situation.* With negative power there is a feeling of resentment and anger that someone has control over you. However, you can alter a negative power balance by asserting yourself. *No one can better control your life than you.* Approach each encounter with that knowledge and assumption. Make sure your voice is strong at the end of statements and doesn't go up in volume or pitch. A statement in which your voice rises up at the end (like a question) comes off sounding like you are asking for approval. It carries no authority.

Stressed? Resentful? Well, As Long As You're Happy...

Any circumstance in your life can be changed. You just have to be ready to accept responsibility for the consequences. A woman once told me how much she hated holidays. Everyone came to her house. She ran around preparing all the food, cleaning the house, making things perfect only to have people complain about everything. My recommendation: Stop hosting the holidays or tell everyone that it will be a buffet and ask what they would like to bring. Her response: "I couldn't do that. People would be upset. I would never hear the end of it." Hear that? What is she *really* saying? "I choose to be miserable during the holidays because it's better than having people mad at me."

Until she can accept that people will be upset with her, that she might have to take some flak, she will be neither free nor happy. She has allowed everyone else to control her.

When Diplomacy Doesn't Work, Sometimes You Have To Be A Conscientious Objector

Who in your life do you allow to upset you? Think how important it is to have that person in your life. If they are not very important, drop that person from your life. Quit beating your head against the wall. This may sound cold, but it is in fact a kindness—both to you and to those you love.

Wouldn't you rather expend your energies on positive relationships instead of squandering them on people that really aren't necessary or meaningful to you? If it *is* important to have that person in your life, (say the person is your mother) then redefine *how* you want that person in your life and what behavior you need to change to make it work.

For example, your mother is an important person in your life. You don't want to drop her because of one area of contention, such as her continual nagging about your weight. Focus your conversations with your mother on the positive. Then, when she hits on the subject of weight simply say pleasantly but firmly, "I would prefer that we don't discuss my weight anymore," and then change the topic. If this doesn't work, tell your mother that it upsets you and that the next time it is brought up you will walk away. Then, keep your promise! After a few times, she will learn to stop. Or if she doesn't, at least you'll be out of earshot!

The Power Grid—Recognizing The Components Of Positive And Negative Power

Positive power comes from within. It starts quietly and then begins to grow, nurtured by a healthy self-esteem. Don't mistake positive power for confidence. Confidence can be present even when self-esteem is low. How can that be?

High Confidence Vs Low Confidence

Well, let's look at Bill, a successful businessman, making $300,000 a year. Bill is great at closing deals and jets around the country putting deals together. He has to have his hands in everything and barks orders. He gets upset at little things, when his desk is not in order or when dinner is not on the table on time. He's driven to keep gathering facts to use not as tools, but weapons, so he can out-talk and out-think his opponent. He rarely has time for social niceties unless they can advance his career.

Bill is a classic example of high confidence. He's great at doing his job, very competent. But he has low self-esteem; he has to make others feel inferior in order to feel good. He cares less for people than he does for getting the job done.

High Self-Esteem Vs Low Self-Esteem

People with high self-esteem feel good about who they are and what they do. They don't compete with others to be number one. They compete against themselves and always strive to be the best.

They are competitive, yet friendly. They admit when they make mistakes. They are positive power people.

Check Yourself

Do a quick check to see if you have high confidence/low self-esteem or high confidence/high self-esteem.

High Confidence/ Low Self-Esteem	High Confidence/ High Self-Esteem
• People think you are egotistical.	• People respect and admire you.
• You never have time for others unless they serve a purpose for you.	• You take time to develop others.
• You see people as road blocks.	• You see people as helpers.
• Your goal is to win-to get what you want. The opposite of win is lose.	• Your goal is to attain the best result.
• You want all the credit.	• You want to share credit with those that helped.
• You try to find out who screwed up so someone can be blamed. You make sure upper management knows who made the mistake.	• You try to find the mistake and how to correct it. You accept responsibility for your area.
• You operate as a separate entity.	• You feel a part of the team.
• You feel a responsibility solely to yourself.	• You feel a responsibility to yourself and to society.

You can be successful with confidence alone. You can have a lot of power too. But the high confidence/high self-esteem person goes beyond mere power to fulfillment. People will want to help you achieve success if you help them feel good about themselves. Wouldn't power and success be even better if it weren't necessary to be adversarial?

Go For The High

High self-esteem people are willing to give power to others because they don't feel threatened. They are less interested in power and more interested in results. And that's what Outcome Thinking™ is all about, results!

Stop and think the next time you are talking with a person. Are you adding value to that person? Are you making them feel good about themselves? If not, what can you say that makes them feel good? Do you point out the positives or the negatives? Often if a person is feeling dumped on in their life they will then dump negatives on someone else in order to feel better about themselves.

TAKE ACTION—Making The Tough Choices
It's easy to acknowledge that we must eliminate negativity from our lives. It becomes much more difficult when the negativity comes packaged as a friend, relative or co-worker. Freeing yourself from such people is really hard to do, but absolutely necessary. Why? Because you become like those with whom you surround yourself. You cannot focus on the positives if you are immersed in negativity.

When Saying No Is The Most Positive Path

This is a painful process. I know from personal experience. I had a friend that I had known for 13 years. We'd had some wonderful times. She was great fun and very social, always getting everyone together to do things. But sadly, she grew catty and gossipy; she enjoyed talking negatively about people that weren't present.

At first, I dealt with her negative talk by simply walking away when she started cutting other people down. After a while I realized that even walking away was not enough. It seemed that there was always someone annoying her. Well, you guessed it. Pretty soon, it became my turn to be the one that annoyed her. I didn't agree with the backstabbing, she didn't want to stop the backstabbing so we stopped being friends.

Did it hurt? Yes. But I now see the pain as "growing pains." One thing I really value is friendship and I believe that friends defend each other. But this woman would cut a friend down behind her back and then be sweet to her face. That alone savages the definition of friendship.

I believe you need to be direct with a person that upsets you, not try to get everyone on your bandwagon. My friend is a good example of low self-esteem. With low self-esteem we try to get people to agree with our viewpoint and to tell us we are right. This results in gossip and negative emotions.

I had to make a decision about my values- did I want to be friends with someone who gossiped or spoke negatively about others? That answer for me was simple: no.

Surround Yourself With
Positive People And Replace Negative With Positive

> ### TAKE ACTION
> Make a list right now of all the positive people in your life. Make a list of all the people you would like to get to know better. Then make a list of the negative people in your life. Start figuring out how you can attract more of the positive people in your life and reduce the negative. Remember some negative people can turn around and become positive. And sometimes you may be drawing the negative out in someone else. So don't just drop everyone cold turkey.

It is also your responsibility to be pro-active in seeking the positive, and in sharing it with others as well when you discover it. Imagine this: you and your co-workers gossip negatively about your company president? Then later you find out you misjudged her?

After having a chance to work more directly with her you see her vision for the company, and you realize that she is both competent and open to listening to ideas. You gain new respect for her, but now you are uncomfortable going to lunch with your co-workers because you no longer share their criticisms.

You now have a responsibility. Remember that you were a part of the negative talk to begin with. It is your job to share your insights and then say you are uncomfortable talking negatively about her. Don't be judgmental of the group. They may not have had the chance to see the side of the president that you have. If things don't change you can choose to stop having lunch with the group. But there is a good chance that you will influence the group to see differently.

Mental Pictures: Self-Portraits

Chiseled In Stone Or A Mural?

When you think of yourself, what comes to mind? We all carry a mental picture of ourselves around with us. This mental picture defines our comfort zone. Everything you do in life you judge against your comfort zone. If it fits your comfort zone—your mental picture of yourself—then you are fine with it. If it does not fit your comfort zone, then you try to sabotage it, either consciously or subconsciously.

Let's say, for example, that you're in sales and you feel you are a $50,000 a year income person. You land a large account and by September you have already reached your commission goal of $50,000. You now have two choices. You can either change your mental picture of yourself and stretch to a new goal or you can keep your old picture of $50,000. Now if you keep your old picture, you might take more time off to be with your family, improve your golf game, or take that long vacation you always wanted. Or, you might coast, calling on present customers rather than calling on new accounts, and taking longer lunch breaks. Your mind will justify all of these things as the right thing to do, because they are consistent with your self-portrait. You see, sometimes you may sabotage your own growth. You may *say* you want to grow to be a $100K a year person, yet you refuse to delegate. That does not square with your mental image. So to change that, you need to begin delegating.

A Work In Progress

Changing your picture of yourself is not as hard as it may seem. Think of one of your successes. That success changed your mental picture of yourself ever so slightly, didn't it? Once your comfort zone is stretched it does not go back.

When Your Self Portrait Changes Over Time

One fun thing I do at corporate seminars is an exercise where everyone writes down one thing about themselves that no one else knows. Then we try to match the statement to the person. This usually results in hilarity as well as insight. People have shared everything from their first jobs as chicken pluckers to a big burly guy who admits to sleeping with the night light on! Aside from learning new things about each other, we learn new things about ourselves. Why don't other people know this about us?

Sometimes the information revealed is a personality change. One woman wrote that she was very shy and never had a date all through high school. Well, no one guessed she wrote that because she was known as the office socialite! She had decided that she didn't want to be shy anymore and worked hard at talking with others and stretching her comfort zone. After a while her actions matched her new picture of herself.

TAKE ACTION: Creating A Snapshot Of Yourself

Take some time to paint your self-portrait with words. Write down how you view yourself. Be candid in your evaluation. Step back and be objective in your appraisal. Write down all the good and all the things you aren't wild about when you think of yourself.

Next write down how you would *like* to view yourself. Go back to your original list and see what things you need to change in order to fit your new view of yourself. For example, let's say your first appraisal of yourself was as follows:

Extroverted. Friendly. Opinionated. Fast to anger. Logical. Focused. Positive. Comfortable at $50K. Good friend. Good listener. Perfectionist. Procrastinator.

Who's That Person In The Picture? You!

The picture you want of yourself is as follows:

Extroverted, but with less assertion of my opinion at all times. Friendly. Slow to anger. Logical. Focused. Positive. $100K person. Good friend. Good listener. Doer—not a perfectionist.

This is the picture you would present and say to yourself every day. You would do everything in accordance with this new portrait. For example, you would look at how many new accounts you need to call on to reach $100K and then every day call on those accounts first. You would stop yourself from stating your opinion about everything and instead train yourself to ask, "What are your thoughts on this?"

You'd Never Recognize Me From My Old Pictures

It is hard to change, but it is also very possible and very rewarding. I know because I changed. I grew up in a family that was very feisty and talkative. Our dinner conversations were lively and often went up several decibels. My husband, Paul, used to joke that he needed to take Tylenol after visiting for dinner. Paul's Dad would sit amazed that we could all talk so loud and have so many stories going at once and still keep up with all of them.

Well, the good thing about our style was that no subject was taboo. I learned that adults didn't always make the best choices and that children could teach adults too. I also came to believe that the louder, funnier and more persuasive my speech was, the better I was as a communicator. I was very opinionated and full of facts on everything, and in the context of dinner with my family, it worked great.

Gradually though, over the years and through my jobs, an awareness began in me. I noticed that I won business negotiations, but I wasn't building long term relationships. I also noticed that people either really liked me or disliked me.

My awareness built over several years, as I paid attention to the little things as well. I remember when Paul and I were driving, I would tell him where to turn even if I wasn't sure where I was going. Of course, we'd then get lost. Every time, Paul would just say, "I know you believed you were right." I came to realize how obnoxious I must have been. I decided that I wanted to change how I communicated.

My How You've Changed!

I wanted to see myself as calm, logical, involving of others, a good listener and fair. I practiced asking other people questions and restraining myself during a conversation. I counted to ten instead of instantly responding to something that was said.

People were used to coming to me for answers since I always had a ready opinion and knew something about everything. I tell you it was hard to give up solving other people's problems because it was a stroke to my ego. With this one, I had to practice listening and then responding with a question instead of an opinion. "Well, what are your thoughts on this?" "Which way do you lean towards and why?" And lastly, the only thing I would allow myself to comment on was my own experience.

For example, if you had come to me for advice on a job that you wanted, the "old me" would have told you *exactly* what to do—no ifs, ands or buts about it. The "new me" would now ask you questions such as, "What do you want to do with the new job? What approaches have you come up with? Why don't you think that approach would work? Would your boss or previous boss be supportive and write a recommendation letter? Would you like me to look over your resumé and cover letter when they're done? Would you like to see copies of good cover letters and resumés I have received?"

The second approach encourages people to take more ownership in their decisions. There is a lot more pride and confidence in the decision. There is also more value added to the person since there is an assumption that they can solve their own problem. In the first scenario, if you don't take my advice it creates an awkwardness for us. You feel obligated to tell me why you didn't take my advice rather than just telling me what you did do. Plus, if you do take my advice and it flops, you'll either blame me and be resentful, or make me the scapegoat.

Of course, friends still come to me for advice. But now they come to bounce ideas off of me to help them make decisions— they don't look for me to give them all the answers. A funny thing has happened; I am learning a lot from others. I am finding out how much more I have to learn and how little I know.

Detour: Comfort Zone Ahead
••••••••••••••••••••••••••••

In order to grow and change your comfort zone, you need to repeat to yourself over and over your new image of yourself. The difference between your actions and what your subconscious mind believes is what motivates you. So as your subconscious mind hears more and more about the person you desire to be, the more your subconscious mind will try to get your actions to be in line with that view point.

TAKE ACTION

In order to best change the view you have of yourself, I recommend that you pick one thing you can do to move out of your comfort zone. Practice it 2-3 times daily until it becomes comfortable for you. Keep stretching yourself!

When I first started public speaking, I knew I would be travel-ing across the United States and constantly speaking to strangers. I wanted to become comfortable talking with anyone, and I wanted to always focus on the positives people have to offer. So I decided to move out of my comfort zone by complimenting three strangers daily.

The first time I tried it was in the parking lot of a grocery store. I spotted a woman about sixty-five. She had her hair freshly done, glasses on a pearl chain, and she wore a matching cream ensem-ble—cream sweater, cream leggings and cream shoes with little bows. She walked with a little bounce and looked just elegant. I stopped her and told her I thought she looked really attractive. Well, she let go of her cart to give me a runway pirouette; I chased for the cart as it headed for the nearest car. She continued the fash-ion show and we both made each other's day! It was a hoot!

I am now very comfortable talking with strangers no matter where I am. Matter of fact, I have a golf league that started with four people and has swelled to over twenty women—many of whom I met just by going up and talking with them. A stranger is just a friend you haven't met yet!

Stuff You Can Try

So what can *you* do to stretch your comfort zone? Here are a few ideas to try:

You Are	You Want To	Move Out Of Your Comfort Zone:
Introverted	Speak up more	Choose where to go to lunch.
		Select what movie to see.
		Give your opinion when you would normally keep it in.
		Speak up in company meetings.

You Are A	You Want To	Move Out Of Your Comfort Zone:
Perfectionist	Be a Doer	Touch each piece of paper only once.
		Make quick decisions. Set deadlines and stick with them.
		Force yourself to delegate and give the other person freedom to do the project in his or her own way.

You Are	You Want To	Move Out Of Your Comfort Zone:
Shy	Be Assertive	Talk to three strangers a day.
		Go to a museum or art gallery by yourself.
		Invite someone from work to lunch.

These are just a few ways you can stretch your comfort zone. Don't try them all at once—just try one until you're comfortable with it. Be sure to reward yourself when you do something well. I recommend that you keep track of your progress in your success log. It is fun to see how much you change over time, and the steps you took to get there.

Stress And Your Comfort Zone

Stressful situations can put us in overdrive. We react rather than think about what we are going to do or say.

TAKE ACTION

Stop right now and write out how you respond to stressful situations. Do you get angry? Take flight? Fight back? Become defensive? Shut down? Try to think of all of your physical body reactions, too. Do you get timid and pull back? Do you slump your shoulders or break eye contact? Do you jut your chin out?

Now go back and write out how you would *like* to see yourself respond during a stressful situation. Do you want to be calm? Feisty? Introspective? Whatever it is you want to be, start acting like you *are* that way. If you become angry or defensive quickly, start saying you are calm and give yourself to the count of ten to respond. Do this daily so you are prepared with how to respond when a stressful situation does arise.

Stress And Your Self-Image

It's Bad Enough When Your Grandma Drags Out Your Grade School Pictures... But Now You're Doing It Too!

During times of stress we usually regress to the self-image we had at age twelve! That is why sometimes you say or do the stupidest things during a fight and you wonder, "Why did I do that?" We tend not to be rational during stressful times.

There are times people will attack you and you will not be prepared to respond. Say you have a heavy workload and you are suddenly asked to take on an extra project. Trying to be gracious, you get it done even though you really need more time. Your boss comes back livid that it was done wrong and chews you out in front of everyone. You are shocked, angered and upset.

Naturally, your first tendency might be to think, "That's not fair! I rushed to meet your deadline" or "I can't believe you would blow up at me in front of everyone. Don't you realize how much I do for you?"

It's natural to want to yell back, but realize that would be detrimental to your career. Yet if you don't say anything you will probably be steamed about it for days and it will build a wall between you and your boss. The resentment may fester and actually sour you on the company.

Choose The Best Time For The Best Effect

In this situation it is not enough to call up a positive mental picture. Sometimes it is too hard to think quickly of a response. Your body is either in flight or fight mode. So just as a professional photographer needs time to adjust the lighting for the picture, you also need to adjust the mood in order to best respond. And since you can't take back what you say it is important that you take the time you need before you respond.

I recommend that in these kinds of situations you take a deep breath, look at the person, and say, "I can see you are very upset. I would like to discuss this with you, but I'm not prepared. Would you be available in thirty minutes?" (or whatever time you need).

This allows you to gather your thoughts and your composure, and to select your words carefully. Remember to assume the best and to talk from the other person's perspective.

Let's Play This Out
•••••••••••••••••••••
Let's take the above situation. You take your time to cool down. So how do you approach your boss? Well, first think about it from your boss's perspective. Here are some possible viewpoints you can take:

Your boss...

1. Doesn't realize how many projects you are doing
2. Over-promised what the company could deliver
3. Had a bad day at home
4. Is feeling pressured himself, and transferring it to you
5. Has low self-esteem

Above all, think about the result you want! Is what you want a good working relationship and the security of knowing that you won't be yelled at for things not under your control? Now it is time to approach your boss.

Prepare yourself to present in a calm and controlled, professional manner. Walk in with great posture and begin something like this: "I realize that having the project done incorrectly really upset you. It upsets me too. I want our area to look good. I currently have five key projects I am working on and I tried to squeeze that one in when I really needed more time to do it properly. So this doesn't happen in the future, what are your ideas on how to best handle it? Would you prefer I stop and tell you what I'm working on so we can reprioritize, that I tell you when I would be able to get to it and how long I think it will take, or that I delegate it to someone else? I would like to do what is most effective for you."

If you are in the habit of saying, "No problem," why are you disappointed when your boss believes you? Many bosses I talk with have no idea what projects their employees are working on. Often they delegate projects and then forget what they delegated and to whom they delegated. I recommend that you keep track of monotonous jobs you do that you think could be eliminated. For your boss, this task may be a "nice to have," not a "need to have." It just may get eliminated from your pile!

A good example of this is the customized handouts I provide for my presentations. I had developed a system for designing new handouts that was fast for me but slow for my staff. It wasn't until they pointed out to me how long it took to develop each handout that I became aware of the inefficiency. From there we devised a new system that sped it up for them and kept the pace I needed. Assume your boss is on your side, and may be merely ignorant of a situation, or what is involved in a particular process.

When You Can No Longer See Where You Fit In The Picture...

Now some of you are rolling your eyes at me, visualizing the boss yelling at you. You're thinking, "Right, I am going to tell my boss I need time to think and get back to him. There is no way he would stand for that. He would just keep on yelling at me."

If that is the situation, then you have to make some choices. One is, do you want to work in that environment? If you do, then you need to accept that your boss is like that and let it roll off your back. Or you can address your boss in a positive way and say, "I want to do the best job possible and make our area look good. Yelling at me in front of everyone throws me off and I feel I don't perform as well for you as I can. What do you need from me in order to not have that happen anymore?" Then try to lay out specifics. Often a boss yells at you if they feel they can. I personally recommend getting out of that situation because it will eventually take a toll on your self-image. Besides, remember what we said about eliminating negativity? It may seem like a reckless, drastic step, but it may be your *best* option.

I should know. I've been there, done that. When I was a retail buyer, I worked for one boss who was great. He really let me explore and do my own thing. Then we got in a new president whose sole concession to employee relations was inviting you to lunch. He seemed to enjoy looking for what you did wrong instead of looking for the right. He would even ask the sales consultants what they didn't like about what you were doing. Feedback is one thing—specifically soliciting negatives is another!

It was interesting to see the entire atmosphere of the organization change under his leadership. People began to blame each other and point fingers. We became short and snapped at each other. Laughter was rare in the halls. And the look of fear crossed our faces when we heard he was in our area. Many of the best and most creative mavericks at our company bailed. They all saw it was his way or the highway.

I stood up to him once and he chewed me out royal. Called me a "gutless buyer" when I told him I didn't agree with his thoughts on a trend. I told him the trend would sell in A & B stores, but not in the little C stores. He said all sixty stores could sell it.

Well, guess what? Only the A & B stores could sell it. When I ran into him later to discuss it, his response was that since I as the buyer was never behind the trend, why would it work? That's when I knew it was time to get out. I wasn't having any fun any more. I was bringing work home because I *had* to rather than because I wanted to. I too had started laying blame, looking for who made the mistake rather than seeking to find the best way to do things. I began to be distrustful and to second guess myself. Leaving was one of the best decisions I ever made.

After six months I went back for a visit. I can't tell you how many people commented on how good I looked—my face looked so relaxed! I hadn't realized how pinched my face had become at work. I vowed then never to let another person affect my attitude again. I decided I would walk away before I let someone eat away at me like that. I chose to care about me as much as I did for my job. Make sure *you* always take care of yourself!

Self-Image Reflects On Everyone

This lesson etched itself into my mind; I would hold on to that unpleasant experience only as a reminder of what not to do when I was a boss. The bosses I worked the hardest for were the ones that gave me the most freedom, who trusted me to make the right choice.

As a kid, did you ever hold a mirror at an angle to the sun and burn a hole in something? Or have you ever used mirrors to add dimension or lighting to a room? Well just like mirrors our self-image can come back to us too, for good or bad. What image do you send to others?

When you think about it, it's the little things that people do that get you to appreciate them and work hard for them. When I worked for a department store, I had a divisional supervisor who was a workaholic and loved to let you know. She would leave notes on your desk with the time 7 a.m. or 6 p.m. so you knew she had been there well before or after office hours. Those notes made me feel awful, like I wasn't doing my job well. I can't help but suspect that that was the whole intent of her little messages.

Heidi, on the other hand, was a great boss. She took me out to lunch on my first day so she could get to know me better. When she learned I was a golfer, she encouraged me to take off a day and join the company golf outing. When I told her I didn't have any vacation time since I had only been on the job one week, she told me she knew I would make up the time some other way. We never counted vacation days, sick days, or clock-watched with each other. We just did what it took to get the job done. I would cancel or change plans if I thought she needed my help because I knew she would let me take what time I needed later without making a big stink over it. I can't say I have ever enjoyed working for someone as much.

All of her actions showed her belief in me. I knew what had to be done and when it had to be done, but the rest was up to me. She knew I would put in time at home or on weekends if that's what it took.

She brought me to every meeting. She never withheld information, or pulled rank and privilege. Instead, she fed me information so I could answer any question in her absence. She did everything she could to give me access to everything she had access to. Then she held me responsible for that trust and privilege.

When you work with someone like this, you can really sail as a team. So often we are reluctant to give others power because we mistakenly feel it will strip us of our own power. Give it away. It comes back to you tenfold. Hold people accountable for the privilege of having information, power and trust. Take it seriously.

Caveat: Sharing information on salaries is not an area for discussion. That is an abuse of privileged information, and not responsible information exchange.

Just imagine if you owned a company, and you really felt that someone was deserving of a raise. So you bumped their salary. Then you find out they are telling everyone how much they make. How does that make you feel? It doesn't entice you to give them any more money or power, does it? Who wants someone on their team that could start a mutiny? Moreover, it's a betrayal of an implied confidence, and highly unprofessional. Always keep quiet about your income! It gives your company incentive to give you more money. Besides, it's the right thing to do.

Paradigms: Limitless Possibilities Or Possibilities Limited?

Paradigms are the way you view things. They are based on your perceptions and your perceptions are based on your actual and learned experiences. Paradigms can limit the way you think and stop you from experiencing things fully.

Here are some examples of paradigms in our culture from Chicken Soup for the Soul, by Jack Canfield & Mark Victor Hansen.

In 1899 Charles Duell, the commissioner of the U.S. Patent Office asked President McKinley to close the patent office. He said, "Everything that can be invented has been invented." Can you even imagine the inventions we would have missed? The space shuttles, computers, the Internet, bread makers, digital clocks, 3M Post it® notes, or, heaven forbid, microwave ovens! Thank goodness McKinley didn't listen.

Western Union is quoted as saying, "This telephone is of no inherent importance to us." They thought it would be here today and gone tomorrow. We laugh looking back now. Yet, I can't tell you how many companies tell me they are not on the Internet because they think it is just a fad. They believe business will continue as it currently is.

In 1981 Bill Gates said, "640K hard drive ought to be enough for anybody." And Tom Watson, chairman and CEO of IBM in 1943 said, "I think there is a world market for maybe five computers." Even the computer gurus underestimated the power of the computer on today's business world.

Today we can't imagine such statements, yet at the time, they seemed wholly reasonable and factual. All of these statements were based on limited information, the paradigms of the times. The moment you assume you know all there is to know on something is the minute you know little. A favorite statement of mine is "The more indispensable you think you are to a company, the more dispensable you are. The more dispensable you think you are, the more indispensable you become."

In today's competitive market you need to have an edge. A natural edge you can give yourself is to think of yourself as a learning sponge. Try to absorb as much as possible. Then try to look at new ways of putting things together. This combination is where most of our inventions come from. Velcro® was created after a man walking his dog through the woods noted how burrs would stick in his dog's fur. Upon returning home, instead of being ticked about having to pull out all these burrs, he started thinking about what made them stick to the fur. This natural curiosity, coupled with creative thought on how it might make things easier, led to the invention of Velcro®. Today Velcro® is used in everything from shoes to upholstery. All because of one person's curiosity.

Why We Have Paradigms

One reason we cling to paradigms is because we crave stability, and we most often look for stability outside of ourselves. You have probably noticed that everything I am talking to you about is based on building security from within. So far we have discussed gaining security and control by utilizing positive self-talk, recognizing your successes and your strengths, building positive power, and breaking out of paradigms. All of these skills change the focus from outside of you to inside of you.

The beauty of this is that the one thing you have complete control over is you! Once you focus your information on having you grounded then you are able to handle many changes in your life. This is important because if you can't handle change in your life, you will have a hard time positively communicating with a person during a stressful time. You will react more to external things that might hurt or upset you.

All of our vulnerability comes from what we think others might be thinking of us. Then we magnify that until it consumes us. We stop trying to do things differently for fear we will rock the boat or be called "different." We pick on people who do things differently. (Until they accumulate wealth. Then that seems to legitimize the person.)

So how do you break out of paradigms and try new things? How do you know if you are stuck in a paradigm? And how do you become more creative?

Break The Mold
• •
How Do You Know If You're Stuck In A Paradigm?

Look around at what you do every day. What things do you do just because you have always done them that way? Are there different ways to do what you do? What could be done to improve how you do it?

For example, in the speaking industry you typically work through Speakers Bureaus that book you and take a 25% commission, or through meeting planners that book events. But I wanted to develop a solid local base of companies that would have me back again and again. So I went directly to the presidents of companies and talked to them about what we could do for their company. I did package pricing for quarterly events and sometimes even tradeouts.

These ideas allowed companies to test us out and see if we delivered what we said we could. Once they saw that we did, they were more than happy to pay full price and work with us on an ongoing basis. This kind of thinking required going outside the box and being creative with possible solutions. I talked to one company for two years before they ever hired me to do a program. Now they have me back every quarter at full fee to train their people.

Now, I was always told this method would not work. I was told that if you ever cut fee and people get wind of it they will get upset.

I was told that if a company hired you for less than your fee they would never want to pay your full fee. If I had listened to that advice I wouldn't have my top four clients. All of them were skeptical of what Impression Management could do for their company and didn't want to invest in it. Today, they all believe in its impact and know it is an investment they can't afford not to make!

Routinely Look At Your Routines

Break out of paradigms and simplify any routine you do. Think like a computer or systemizer and see how you can "duplicate" yourself by allowing others to do what you do. In my office, we sit down quarterly and look at what is consuming the largest amount of our time and what we can do to make it easier. Years ago, we found that we spent a lot of time packing for each speaking engagement and checking that we had everything. When we hit months of a dozen or more speeches it was just too much to handle.

So we created a speaker's checklist, a master sheet of everything I could possibly want to bring to a speech. This master checklist would come to me first with the client company's name, speech title, date and time. I would create the handouts to go with that company's program, check off the items I needed and pass the list on to the person packing me for that speech. All visual materials we created were marked and put on a sheet so we could refer to them by number. This whole new system allowed us to do four times as many speeches with less stress. *We took the guess work out of the communication.*

TAKE ACTION

Stop right now to take a minute to look at how your time plays out. List the activities you do in a week and how much time you estimate you spend in each area. Then look at what things you think drive your company or area. Look for things that will set you apart. Note what percentage of your time should be spent in those areas. Now compare the two lists and start looking at ways to eliminate things that are routine and don't allow you to excel.

For example, let's imagine that your week is spent something like this:

Meetings	35%
Calls on potential clients	30%
Paperwork on sales	20%
Drive time to appointments	10%
Mail, etc.	5%

Your pay and recognition comes from the following:

New accounts	50%
Building existing accounts	30%
Meetings (where you get new information to sell clients)	15%
Misc.	5%

Systemize

Keep Track To Stay On Track

Now look for ways to systemize or eliminate doing things that are not revenue producing. Is there a way you can cut down on the paperwork? Can you do it all at the end of the day to save time? Can you do it between calls and fax it in? Can the company reduce the amount of paperwork needed for a sale? Can they be more computerized? Does it make sense for you to hire someone to help you with the paperwork? Look at the drive time. Could you plan to do territories and better schedule calls to clients or potential clients? Look at the meetings. What is productive about them? How can you expand on that and get rid of some of the unproductive meeting time? If you aren't the manager, make suggestions on what can be done to improve the meetings.

Now, what if you are not in sales? What if you are an assistant or an administrator? The same principle applies. Make your lists again and look at what can be systemized. For example, let's say the person you are working for is constantly in meetings. Look at making a checklist for them of what they might need from you for upcoming meetings. Ask for the list back by 1 p.m. the day prior so you can pull everything together at your leisure.

Look for ways you can make things easier. If they are always asking you to write letters to people for birthdays, or a letter of thanks for interviews, take some time to do a shell letter that they approve. Then you can use that shell each time. Just remember, if something seems complicated to you, it probably is.

I recommend that after you have made your list of how you think you spend your week, that you actually track your week to see if you are correct. You will be *very* surprised! Sometimes we spend time on things we aren't even aware of. Using this technique and reviewing it every quarter has allowed me to grow the business, cut down my hours and reduce my stress. Remember to do this every quarter to ensure you keep fresh.

So Once You've Made Your List
How Do You Stay Creative With Solutions?

Get Creative

Start thinking about where you are the most creative. Morning? Afternoon? In your office? Your car? Your home? On a walk? Do you need to be facing out a window? At a wall? My energy is highest in the morning, in my car, or at my office looking out a window without any phone distractions. So quarterly in the morning at my office I reflect on what things can be done differently. How can things be simplified? Where is my time most productive?

TAKE ACTION

First, brainstorm and list as many ways you can think of to do a project differently. Remember no idea is a bad idea. It is more important to list as many as possible than to list only the practical. Once you have your list, go back and think how you would implement the idea to achieve the desired result. For example, let's say a lot of your time is spent in meetings. Some of your brainstorm solutions might be:

Send others to meetings

Skip meetings

Put more on paper

Use internal e-mail and have fewer meetings

Prioritize meetings

Hold meetings during my slow time—late afternoon

Now look at ways you can implement some of these ideas. For example, could information be dispensed ahead of time on the internal e-mail system so people could respond to it? Could departments rotate taking that responsibility? Can you attend the top meetings and groom others to go to some of the other meetings? Could you prime them on the key information to bring back so you can take action? This is a great way to get team involvement and interaction. *Keep your mind open to solutions.* Video conferencing is a great way to go if your offices have people in different areas.

Think Outside The Box:
How Do You Break Out Of Paradigms?

First, stop accepting them as the absolute truth. Look for ways around them even if your new ideas sound ridiculous. I remember hearing about a phone company that was having a terrible time with their lines icing over up north. They would send repair people in to climb the poles and chip the ice off the lines. The repair people were being attacked by polar bears and didn't want to go up north to repair lines anymore. The phone company had a dilemma, as they needed to keep the lines free of ice but they didn't know how.

They had a big brainstorming meeting. They talked about making the poles out of different material, putting spikes in them, sending in a search party to hunt the polar bears, etc. Finally one woman raised her hand and said, "I was a nurse in the Vietnam War and I remember the helicopters coming in with the wounded. The wind and engine heat was so intense you couldn't get close to the helicopter. And I was wondering, couldn't we just send helicopters up to fly over the lines and wouldn't the heat and the wind velocity knock the ice off the lines?" That is what they do today. It saves them millions of dollars. One idea implemented in a whole new way.

What Stops Us From Thinking Outside The Paradigms?

Since early childhood we are often taught that failure is bad. We learn that no one remembers who took second place at the Super Bowl and we certainly don't cheer on a team that has lost for several years in a row. Even when kids play their games during recess, many play to win, not just to have fun. We become conditioned to get A's or B's.

Don't get me wrong. Winning is good. So is getting good grades. What I don't like is that losing is put in the sole context of "bad." Why? Couldn't it also be a way to test techniques and strategies to get better results?

Redefine Failure

Try thinking of your failures in a whole new way. Try to celebrate the things that go wrong. Don't ask, "What went wrong or who screwed up?" Instead ask, "What do we need to do differently to make this work?" Some of our best creators are people who were thought to be failures in their times. Listen to some of these "failures" as shared in *Chicken Soup for the Soul* by Jack Canfield and Mark Victor Hansen:

- Henry Ford failed and went broke five times before he finally succeeded.

- Babe Ruth held the record for the most home runs, but he also holds the record for the most strikeouts.

- Comments on Fred Astaire's first screen test were "Can't act! Slightly bald! Can dance a little!"

- Walt Disney was fired by a newspaper editor for lack of ideas. He also went bankrupt several times before he built Disneyland.

- Louisa May Alcott, the author of *Little Women*, was encouraged to find work as a servant or a seamstress by her family.

• Abraham Lincoln had two nervous breakdowns before he became President. He became so broke trying to get into office (he had several failed attempts to get into the Senate) that his wife tried pawning his monogrammed shirts on street corners.

Anything Worthwhile Entails Risk

So, failure is what *you* make of it. You have to decide you are ready to take the risk and try something new. You have to decide that it is better to take a risk and know the answer than live through the "what if." This is not always an easy decision to make. The first time you try it, it can be painful.

I remember in ninth grade deciding that I really wanted to go to an upcoming dance. It was "Sadie Hawkins" where the girls asked the guys. Well, I decided I really wanted to ask Joe, the cute boy with a locker next to mine. He hesitated, but then said okay. Well, I didn't feel like he really wanted to go with me. So I told him to only say yes if he really wanted to go with me, otherwise I would rather he go with someone else. Well, he wanted to go with Cheryl, so that put me at ground zero.

I did have an alternate in mind so I asked him. He was already taken. Now I had a big decision to make. Did I really want to go to the dance bad enough to risk another rejection? I decided I did and with friends picked a few prospects. When all was said and done, I asked six guys and ended up without a date. You can imagine how I felt! I really felt like a loser. Some of the guys had already had dates, but some of the guys said no because they really wanted to go with someone else. I then compared myself to those girls and tried to figure out why the boys would prefer them. *What is wrong with me?* raced through my mind.

I don't know why, but for some reason it just clicked: *I was okay.* Just because they didn't want to go to the dance with me didn't mean that something was wrong with me. I thought of how I had many nice sweaters but I still preferred certain sweaters for no other reason than I just *did.* Liking certain sweaters didn't lessen the value of the other sweaters. The other thing I realized was that at least I knew the answer. I wouldn't spend the rest of my life wondering if I *could* have gone to the dance or if Joe would go with me or not. I knew the answer, I could live with the answer, and could move on from there. The funny thing was that, years later, four of the guys came back and told me they wished they had gone with me. Well, I wish they had too—except maybe I wouldn't have learned what I did.

The One Opinion That Really Matters

That one lesson taught me that what *I* thought was more important than what everyone else thought. The way I viewed that failure would have more of an impact on me than on anyone else. And if I didn't view it as a failure then no one else would either.

They'll Take Their Cue From You

You see people respond more to our reactions than to the information being given. You have complete control over how you respond. Let's say that you are working on a project and suddenly your boss puts in someone to coordinate the whole thing. Everyone really thought you would be tapped for the lead because you had put in the majority of work so far.

A sympathetic co-worker comments, "What a bummer that they didn't give you the position. Doesn't that just tick you off?" You respond, "Yes, I am really angry. They don't even value what I do." Then pretty soon all your co-workers are looking for you to clash with the new person. They will look for the negative angle on anything either you or the new person says. They will try to find ways to validate your perception.

However, if you respond with positives, you'll get positives. "I think it's great they put another set of eyes to keep this project fresh. It really means they value what we are doing here." In your co-workers eyes your value just went up. The company believes in what you are doing so much they will even put extra people on the project. They will look to see what other ways the company values you and they will look to see the signs that you and the new person get along.

Act Like You're In Control And You Are
••

Always think positively and remember how much control you *do* have over any situation, even very embarrassing ones. In the third grade, I went to an all day Girl Scout camp. My Mom was one of the counselors so she was along to run some of the day's activities. We had a free hour and many of us went through a thistle patch to get to some sand and a beach. We were sitting there making sand castles when I really had to go to the bathroom. I pushed it to the limit until I absolutely had to go *that minute.* I got up and started running to the bathroom, which was on the opposite side of the thistle patch, only to realize (painfully!) that I had no shoes on! I decided to try to get to the bathroom, but didn't make it in time. I was devastated. I had never wet my pants in my life and here I was in third grade with wet pants in front of all my friends. I didn't know what to do.

Practically in tears, I found my Mom and begged her to take me home. She explained that she couldn't leave and that I would just have to deal with it. I was now in total tears. I said how humiliated I was and if she was any mother at all, she would spare me the shame and take me home. My Mom looked at me and said, "Anne, I have responsibilities here that I can't walk away from just because you want me to. I realize that right now you are devastated, but the choice is really yours. If you choose to make a big deal out of this everyone will know. But you can also go sit in the sun until it dries and no one will know anything. People will respond in the way you present yourself. So the choice is yours." And she walked away.

I stood for a while sending daggers at her back, but that didn't help. I saw a drinking fountain so I ran over to it with a glass and then "accidentally" spilled the glass on my lap. I sat out in the sun until it dried. My Mom was right. No one knew anything. To anyone that saw me, they thought I had spilled the water in my lap.

I realized then that you can change how people react to an event by how you respond to that event. They will see it as a blessing or a curse depending on how you see it and react to it.

Packaging Is Half The Sale

Just think about it! You have so much control and you might not even realize it. How do you describe your job? Are you "just" a sales person or are you part of building a dynamic organization? Are you "just" a receptionist or are you the ambassador of the organization? Are you "just" a mom or are you a developer of our future generations? People will give your job the same importance as you give it. No more, no less.

Think about this when you are presenting new ideas to people. Keep your enthusiasm high and your energy focused. Keep your voice even and avoid having an upward lilt at the end of your sentence. An upward lilt will make it sound like you are asking approval or asking a question. It will undermine your authority.

Imagine that we are talking about where to go to lunch. I suggest we go to a new Italian restaurant. "You wouldn't want to try that new Italian restaurant across the street, would you? I mean, it might be fun to try something new, don't you think? Otherwise we could go to the pasta place. Where do you want to go?" Now does that inspire you to try that restaurant? Does it even entice you a little? Probably not.

Now what if I said, "I know where we should go to lunch—that new Italian restaurant. I hear they have a fantastic menu and great ambience. It'd be so much fun to try something new. Should we go there?" This creates more excitement, especially if I have an upbeat voice and I phrase my question strongly in the end. This way has you thinking the restaurant might have something new to try and is much more appealing.

How Words Shape Others' Paradigms

What You Say Skews How Others See Things

Look at how you phrase things to others. If you look for the positive, others will look for it also. Just an aside—this also applies to your personal life. I have seen so many people cut down their loved ones and talk about what they don't do well. They focus on what they are not getting from their spouse. This focus begins to grow until it is all you can see in your spouse. I confess I did this for years until I thought about my sister.

I never heard my sister say anything negative about her spouse. Consequently any disputes they had were kept pretty much to themselves. I noticed that I, in turn, always looked for the good things in her husband. Like how he played with the kids, how involved he was with coaching them, and how supportive he was of her love of sewing and even supported buying a $3000 sewing machine. I focused on all the neat things he had to offer.

The Words You Choose Reveal More Than You Know

I noticed how another friend always complained about how her husband wouldn't talk much and how he didn't help with the children very much. Every time we were together, I watched to see if he did talk and if he did help with the children. I looked for his actions to fit what she talked about and consequently, I didn't feel he was a very supportive husband. *Do our words reflect reality or shape reality?*

Your View Shapes Their View

So, what view do you want people to have of your job, your life, and of you? How do you want people to see your spouse? Now I am not saying you should paint a false picture or always paint a rosy picture, especially when you don't feel that way. I am just saying you should realize that what you say and how you say it will affect what people think and feel. You can't just completely cut a person down and then the next day say how wonderful he/she is and expect anyone to be overjoyed for you. They will be thinking, "but isn't this the same person that you hated yesterday?"

As you can see, all of this is pointing towards taking control of your attitude and your thoughts. By taking control of these you begin to be more centrally balanced. You are able to take a few more knocks in life because you find your balance from within rather than from external sources. That way if some part of your life falls apart your whole life won't fall apart.

Watch The Paradigms You Set For Others
· ·

This is a fundamental principle that must be taught to children—especially during the teen years. During that time it is so easy to feel insignificant if you aren't accepted by your peers. You may be an A student, but if you don't get a date you might feel awful about yourself. It is really important to get children to focus on what makes them special and unique. How others value them is a lot less important than how your child values himself/herself.

For workers, it is important that each person feels an integral part of the team, with a clear understanding of their role in shaping the company so they assume responsibility. One of the results of using Outcome Thinking™ is that everyone begins to think "WE" versus "ME." This is the true synergy of a company.

When people focus on the positive they will try to make ideas work. They will look for ways for the company to stand out in a crowd. They will pitch in to get things done. They will look less at what others have and focus more on what they need to do to get things done. They will build each others' self-esteem and be able to spread power around. You won't hear people say, "You have to do that because that's what I had to do when I was in your position."

Passing On The Paradigms—Just "Because"
· ·

I am amazed at how many companies keep policies and procedures in place based on what they had to go through. I have met many managers that hated how management treated them, but then when they are promoted they delegate the same work down with the justification that "I had to do that when I was there." They look at it as a part of their earned right as a manager. Instead they should remember how it made them feel and change the mold. The loyalty would definitely increase. Try to always think from the other person's perspective. What are they thinking and feeling? How can you make things easier?

As a summary of Parts One and Two, with Outcome Thinking™ you always:

◆ Focus on the outcome, not the process.
◆ Think positively from the other person's perspective.
◆ Think outside the paradigms.
◆ Repeat what you heard the other person say before responding.

In order to develop your Outcome Thinking™ style you must practice positive self-talk, recognize your successes and strengths, break out of paradigms, and you must embrace failure. You begin to realize how much control you have over all aspects of your life and you begin to get your personal power and security from within.

PART THREE

Communicating with Outcome Thinking™

Delivery of the Message: Body Language

Self-Talk—People Can Eavesdrop!

Equally as important is the way the message is delivered. We can all think of a time when someone made a comment that was really a zinger in disguise. What was your reaction? What you are really reacting to is the person's body language and voice intonation rather than the message. According to Ray Birdwhistell, over 65% to 90% of all conversation is interpreted through body language and voice intonation! But only about 4% of the population understands how to read body language. Most of us respond in our gut to what a person said, but we are not sure why. Have you ever retold a story to someone only to have them say, "So, I don't get what you are upset about." You finally throw up your hands and say, "You had to be there!"

I once worked with a woman we called "Princess." She flirted with all of the men, but only talked with the women when she wanted something. She reacted to women like they were invading her territory. When I first started, though, I had no idea that she was this way. I would always chat with her in a friendly way. One day in the lunchroom two of the men commented to me that they liked my fuschia blazer just as "Princess" came in. She stopped and said, "What a beautiful colored blazer. I just love the color fuschia." Pausing, she wrinkled her nose and said, "I never would have worn it because it just doesn't seem professional for the office, but you seem to be able to get by with it!" After she left, the guys looked at me and said, "I think you just got complimented and stabbed all at the same time." This was a great case of where the body language and voice intonation spoke louder than the words. The clear underlining message was "You are not very professional in my eyes."

As managers, it is imperative that you be aware of the body language you use and make sure that it is congruent with your message. If you shift your eyes and look away a lot your people will not trust the message being given. If you raise your voice in a question while issuing quotas, it will sound as though you don't believe they are achievable.

When Body Language Changes

In order for your message to be believable, your body language must transmit the same message. Up until age five our body language generally matches our words. After that, you learn that you shouldn't always say precisely what you're thinking. At that point our body language will remain true to our thoughts even if it doesn't match the words we are saying.

Kids Say The Darndest Things

When I was about five, I was out shopping with my Mom. We ran into a woman that tended to be long winded with her stories. At first I was just antsy like a typical five year old. After a while though I had to go to the bathroom. I pulled on my mother's sleeve and said, "Mom." She told me to just wait a minute. I pulled on her again and said, "Mom, I have to go to the bathroom." She told me, "Just a minute, Anne." Now at this point I was shifting foot to foot and literally holding it in. I looked up at the woman and realized that she was nowhere near being done with her story. I remembered a recent dinner conversation and looked at my Mom and said, "But Mom, you don't like her anyway." Boy, did I ever learn, you do not always repeat what you hear at the dinner table!

I learned it was not polite to point out things that seemed odd to me about people. I learned I couldn't just say what I felt. I learned that even if I didn't like the Christmas present I had to say thank you, and point out something I liked about it. I learned I had to hide disappointment or I might hurt others.

When children learn this, their body language remains in synch with their thoughts and feelings, not their words. Therefore, a child might say, "Thank you. I don't have anything in this color," but the eyes will be slightly downcast, shoulders slumped, head slightly tilted and lower lip out a little bit. The body language will show the disappointment even if the words don't.

Is Your Body Language Blabbing Family Secrets?

As we get older, we get a little better at covering up our feelings vocally. We learn to change the direction of the conversation, but our body language still reveals the truth. I remember the Christmas my husband and I separated. It was the first Christmas in fourteen years that I hadn't spent with him. It was particularly hard on me because we had gotten into a routine where we spent Christmas Eve at his parents' house and Christmas Day at my folks' house. Over the years, my brother and sisters also adopted this same tradition of being at their in-laws Christmas Eve and at our folks' house Christmas Day.

Consequently, my parents had their own ritual of spending a quiet Christmas Eve together. But my parents knew I was going to be alone, so they invited me to share Christmas Eve with them. Anticipating my parents' practice of buying one big present for each child and one smaller one, I asked my Mom to just get me a lot of little things instead of one big present so I could feel awash in treasures. I thought it would take my mind off my sadness. Besides, I am really a little kid when it comes to gifts. I just love lots of little packages to open.

That night, I was feeling really lonely and sad. Trying to get me in the spirit of things, my parents exchanged excited looks and said, "Should we have her open THE gift?" After much anticipation, they finally said, "You just have to open this one now." My Dad was particularly excited since, I later learned, it was his idea to get me this gift. I really wanted to have gifts to open on Christmas, but they seemed so excited that I assumed it must be some small gift they thought I would get a kick out of. Well out came this big package.

My heart began to sink. I thought, "Oh no, they got me one big gift and they want me to open it now." But then I thought maybe the package was deceiving. I opened it and nestled inside was a professional Casio piano. My heart just sank. I didn't want it, it didn't make me happy, and worse, I didn't really know why. It should have made me happy—I love music and I missed my piano! I knew how expensive it was, so I knew it was my one big gift. I guess that, being newly single, I didn't want to spend any more time alone in my apartment than I had to. It was just too lonely for me. And to me, the piano meant time alone in my apartment. I know my face showed my disappointment.

At first Mom and Dad were too excited to notice. Mom told me how Dad came home all excited to buy it, but she had discouraged him at first, saying I wouldn't want one because I wouldn't want to sit alone in my apartment. Then she changed her mind when we went to my cousin's Christmas concert, and I whispered to her that I missed my piano. I had given it to my sister to keep after my separation, until I could get a house.

After a short while, my Mom said, "She doesn't like it." Dad dismissed her concerns. "Nonsense" he said. "She just doesn't remember any songs. She loves it." Meanwhile, I was so sad that this was going to be my only gift for Christmas and at the same time I felt just awful about my reaction to this wonderful gift. I knew they thought they had bought me the perfect gift. And I couldn't even fake excitement for them. Besides that I felt selfish since the whole point of Christmas is the giving not the receiving!

Later that night while Mom and I did dishes, she mentioned that I didn't seem too excited. I decided to tell her the truth about how I felt. So I told her how I just didn't want to spend any time in the apartment and that I knew they did it out of love, but would they mind if I returned it? Well, it turned out my Dad had bought it through a friend, so I couldn't return it. Now I really felt terrible because I made my Mom feel bad. Could things get worse? You bet!

The next day, as each person arrived, they asked, "Was she just ecstatic?" My Mom and Dad had told them all about the piano. Then, out came dozens of brightly wrapped packages from under the tree…for me! I felt even worse as I realized they had bought all the little presents I had asked for and the piano was just extra! I was in shock, ashamed and felt very selfish. Even as adults we can't always mask our body language. Sooner or later we reveal our true thoughts.

Why It's Important To Understand Body Language

Once you learn to read body language, you can see what a *person is thinking but not saying.* You can tell when they are in agreement with you, disagreement, bored, interested, upset, angry or confused.

I did some intense studying of body language in order to be able to negotiate better. I had studied the traditional ways of negotiating such as positional bargaining, but found that they didn't give me any insight into the other person. I wasn't finding a way to connect on a deeper level with them. Additionally, most of the people on the other side of the negotiating table were generally twenty years older than me. Even if I became adept at the tactics of traditional negotiating, these people had been doing it for so long they would always be able to outthink me.

Negotiations: Make "I" Contact

I also knew that much of the outcome of the negotiation is based on how you feel about the person and how the negotiation is being handled. I thought back to negotiations where I had agreed to less than I normally would. The common denominator in each instance was the sincerity and great approach of the other person. Instead of thinking about winning—which was ME oriented, I wanted to focus on adding value to the other person and be more WE oriented.

So, that left me with one solution—to understand what my colleagues or adversaries were thinking, but not saying. That way I would know when to make concessions, when to hold, and what questions to ask so we could arrive at the best outcome. Body language can provide those clues while at the same time redirecting your focus from yourself to the other person. You have to listen not only with your ears, but your whole body as well.

Yes, I See What You're Saying

The first time I used Outcome Thinking™ was during a major negotiation with a vendor with whom we did over $12 million in business between two buying areas. We had a major meeting with the president of the company, the sales manager, the salesmen and the management of our company and both of us buyers. At the beginning of the meeting, the vendor's team came in and sat on one side of the table. My colleagues and I sat on the other side of the table.

The most senior buyer started the session by reviewing our joint agenda. As she went through each point I just sat and watched their president. I tried to imagine what he was thinking and feeling by reading his body language.

We had three major points on the agenda:

1. To get more advertising money.

2. To advertise their top shoes in our major sale.

3. To continue to return and receive credit for all shoes we felt were defective. (This included all the shoes that customers returned just because they didn't like them. We knew the vendor had thousands of pairs we had returned to them that they wanted us to take back.)

I watched their president squirm. He switched legs from one side to the next. He adjusted his tie and picked lint off his clothing. He looked at the ceiling. He flipped his tie. He crossed his arms, and uncrossed his arms. He looked at his fingers and drummed them on the table. Finally he took the agenda, flipped it over, crossed his arms and legs and leaned back. At that point, the room got quiet.

As I watched him, I saw from his body language that he was irritated, that he felt attacked and unappreciated. I saw that he felt we were asking for a lot and not giving enough in return. So I leaned forward, looked at him, and said, *"You have built a very successful company in a relatively short amount of time. You found a niche for comfort shoes that may be worn to work. What I want to know is what are your plans for the company in the next five years? How do you plan to advertise and grow and how can we assist you?"*

He looked at me skeptically, leaned forward, and on the back of the agenda sheet started sketching his ideas. The more he talked the more animated he became. I learned he was launching a major advertising campaign that was going to cost him a bundle. He was planning radio, television and billboard advertising. We started talking about how we could link into his campaign. I mentioned that we had three major sales a year and it would be great exposure to get him into those ads. We brainstormed what shoes to put in and decided a family shoe ad would be great. He offered to discount his top two styles for us.

Finally we got to the issue of defective shoes in his warehouse. I remembered how he picked lint off himself (a sign that a person disagrees with what you said, but feels constrained in offering his opinion) while we discussed why we needed him to take the shoes back. So I said, *"We know you build a great shoe and we want to drive your business as much as possible. Your "walk-test" campaign is a great example of your belief in your shoe quality. We also believe the shoes are so good that if people wear them they will like them. So we are willing to have people buy them, "walk-test" them and return them if they don't find them comfortable. We know the risk of returns, but we believe the risk of one return is worth the extra ten pair we can sell using this method. What we need to know is what you would prefer us to do. Should we stop having the stores support your "walk-test" campaign or should we go forward realizing that many of the shoes coming back to you will be due to customer discretionary returns instead of defects?"*

He looked at me and replied that he would rather stand behind the walking program. He would continue to accept the shoes customers returned. He currently had thirty thousand pairs in his warehouse.

When we finished, he laughed, flipped over the agenda, looked at it and said, *"I just gave you more than you came here to ask for and I feel good about it!"*

We all shook hands and as he was about to leave, he stopped, turned around and announced, *"I just think you should know that I came here today to pull your $12 million dollar account. I was so angry I was willing to walk away from our business with you. Instead I am leaving excited about our business with you."*

Adversary To Partner:
Listen With Your Eyes And See With Your Ears

He came in as an adversary and left a partner. Why? Because by using Outcome Thinking™—talking from his perspective—and by reading his body language, I was able to connect with him as a person. The session wasn't about *what can we get*, it was about how we can grow two businesses. If I hadn't been able to read his body language, I wouldn't have known that he was feeling personally attacked about the defective shoes. I wouldn't have known that he was defensive, thinking *we* were saying his shoes were not top quality. And I would have probably approached it all wrong.

From that day on, I have used the ability to read other people's body language in all aspects of my life. Think how much more connected you would be with your boss if she would notice when you are upset and address it immediately. Think how nice it would be if your spouse saw immediately that you had a tough day and asked you about it. Think how nice it would be to recognize when a customer is confused by what you said so you can avoid any misunderstandings.

A Basic Body Language Primer

This skill, when combined with Outcome Thinking™, creates a powerful communication tool. Together we will examine some of the body signs and their meanings.

Before we begin, I do want to caution you:

We will be looking at each sign individually, but body language is ideally read in clusters. This means you have to discern the meaning of all the signs in the context of each other, not just one sign on its own. Think of it kind of like learning a foreign language. The first time you try to put a paragraph together you will probably put the words in the wrong spot. But with practice, you will understand the total meaning and be able to fluently speak the language.

Body language is similar. At first you will be consumed with watching each twitch a person does, after a while you'll be able to see a cluster of signs that tell you how the person is truly feeling rather than relying on just one gesture. Therefore, think of these body signs as guidelines, not absolute truths. Whenever you see a sign you need to stop and ask questions to make sure you are correctly interpreting what the person meant. Body language is tied to our thoughts and not our words. This is why you can sometimes get mixed signals from people. When in doubt listen to the body language, not the words!

Two other things to keep in mind: One, people do not like to be told what they are thinking and feeling. So please do not go up to someone and say, "I know you are angry because you just squinted your eyes." There is nothing more annoying than someone making you feel like you are transparent. Body language is to be used to connect better with others, not to control others.

Two, the body language we are looking at is based on European-American culture. There are differences in every culture. For example, in many Asian countries it is considered rude to make too much eye contact so the eyes are often averted during a conversation. For most European-Americans, averting the eyes is seen as withholding information or being devious. You can see the problem in just simply applying this European-American reading to all cultures. The information offered here is based on the studies of body language experts, including Desmond Morris, Ray Birdwhistell, Alan Pease, and Julius Fast.

Positive Signs:

Head Tilt– This shows interest. Tilt your head while listening. You will find that you will actually become a better listener since your body will trigger your subconscious mind to listen.

Head Nod– Generally this gesture shows that you are listening and generally signals agreement. However this gesture can mean something entirely different for women and men. Many

women nod to signal "I am listening to you" while most men only nod when they are in agreement with you. Why the difference?

To understand this better let's look at some differences in how men and women communicate in general. (I realize not all men or women communicate in a set style. This is just meant to give you an overview of how *most* men and women communicate.)

Gender Differences

John Gray and Debra Tannen each talk about the differences in how men and women communicate. For ease here, I am going to simplify the difference, although please realize that not all men and women fit neatly into categories.

In a nutshell, men communicate with status in mind; they seek to solve problems. Women communicate with connecting in mind. These are two very different ways of communicating and neither way is better than the other. In order to be a more effective communicator, you do need to understand the differences.

Women will often come back to the same issue over and over again, not to find a solution, but just to air their feelings. Men like to bring something up once, resolve it, and move on. Men close that mental file and move on to the next. This difference in communication style can result in women concluding that men are cold and withdrawn while men often find women emotional and irrational.

These differences come through in body language. Women will often nod to show they are listening, not to signal that they are in agreement. Men will generally only nod if they agree with what you are saying. So it is very important that you clarify, with a question, whether or not a person agrees with you. Don't assume the head nod means "Yes"!

Let's look at an example of the difference in the way men and women communicate. Say Susan decides to have a nose operation. She talks it over with her husband, Fred, and he agrees that she should go ahead and do it. Weeks after her surgery, Susan is out shopping with a friend and she passes a mirror. She stops, looks at her face, and says, "You know, I hardly recognize myself. I look in the mirror and I'm not sure who I am anymore." Her friend responds, "I know what you mean. You may have not liked your nose, but it was a part of who you are. It will take some time to get used to." Later on Susan shares her feelings with her mother. Her mother reassures her by saying, "Well, it will take some time to get used to. You do have a new look to your face, but it is still the same you. You will have to give yourself some time."

Susan decides to talk to Fred that night. She passes him the mashed potatoes and she comments, "You know Fred, I look in the mirror and I just don't recognize myself anymore. I look so different." Fred looks at her lovingly and says "If you don't like your nose, why don't you just get it redone?" At which Susan explodes with, "What do you mean 'if I don't like my nose?' You don't like it, do you? Why didn't you just say so from the beginning?" They're both defensive. Susan says, "I don't know why I bother trying to talk with you. You just don't understand." And poor Fred just sits there confused and dazed, thinking, "What did I do wrong?"

From Fred's point of view, Susan presented a problem—she doesn't like her face—and he offered a solution: get your nose redone. Susan wanted to connect—*I feel different. Reassure me that I look okay.* What she heard was—re-do your nose.

In business it is imperative that you try to think from the other person's perspective and communicate from that perspective. That means making sure you are all on the same page and being considerate of where each person is coming from. Realize that most men, being solution based, want the bottom line first and then the details. Most women give the details and then the bottom line. By the time the woman reaches the bottom line, the man is already confused and not sure which details are important and which ones are irrelevant. Consequently, he won't remember *any* of *the details.* He will spend the whole time thinking "Where is she going with this story?"

Enunciate Clearly

I recommend that, for clarity in business, you always mention the bottom line first and then go back over the details. For example, imagine you are working on a major project that is due in the client's hands by the end of the month. Because of a series of delays and crises, you estimate the project will not be ready until the tenth of the next month. Your boss asks how the project is coming along.

A woman might answer with, "Well the materials were three days late getting to us due to a problem at the plant. On top of that, we have had several people out with the flu that's going around and we had to stop the project for a few days when we all worked on the Kensinger project." A man would most likely respond, "I estimate we will not be ready to deliver the project to the customer until the tenth of the next month." He will then launch into the details as the boss asks questions.

Business people are in a hurry and they want the bottom line first. People don't want to get the names of all the people that called, just the ones they need to immediately tend to. They don't want lengthy explanations or excuses, just facts. If you can't deliver right now, when can you deliver? How will you compensate for the delay? Always state the bottom line first, then go back and give the supporting details. People will be prepared to listen to you and will focus on what you have to say rather than trying to figure out what you are leading up to. Of course you need to do all of that with an upbeat friendly tone so you don't come off as bossy or terse.

More Positive Body Language— Position Yourself For Success, Literally!

Smiling– is a positive gesture that relieves tension for both you and others and puts people at ease. It is important that you make eye contact first and then smile. If you are already smiling when you turn to look at someone it doesn't seem sincere to that person. If you look at them and then smile, they feel that what you saw pleased you and so you smiled. An interesting thing about smiling is that you have an involuntary muscle underneath your eye and when you are truly happy that muscle creates a fat fold underneath your eye. It doesn't sound very attractive, but it is—a genuine smile is always more appealing than a fake one.

Dilated Pupils– When you are interested in something your pupils will dilate up to four times their size. This shows excitement and interest. Now most of us instinctively read dilated pupils as more friendly and interested, but we rarely know we are doing it. If during negotiations a person's pupils dilate, it means he's interested in the deal, even if he says he isn't. At that point hold to your original stand and ask him what he likes most about the deal. Conversely, if his pupils contract or do not dilate, you know he's genuinely skeptical of your offer.

Hand on Cheek– This gesture shows evaluation and genuine interest. The person likes what you have to say, is taking it all in, and evaluating it. At this time it's helpful to ask questions to draw the person out and to hear her thoughts.

Chin Stroking– Here the person is making a decision. Don't interrupt! Watch for the body language signal that immediately follows. Does he lean back and cross his arms? Those are "no" gestures. Elicit agreement on points and clarify points of disagreement. If he leans forward, keep quiet and let him talk first.

Seated Readiness– This gesture shows excitement and agreement. This is an excellent posture to take when you are being interviewed since it shows enthusiasm. If this gesture immediately follows chin stroking, it means the person is saying, "yes." At this point when negotiating start using "we" as though you are both in agreement on this issue.

Negative Signs: Objectionable Body Language

The following gestures give a more negative connotation and can put the other person on the defensive. Remember to read the gestures in the cluster in order to not misread what is being said. For example, crossed arms may signal defensiveness, or it may simply mean the room is cold. If the room is cold, the arms will be held tight into the body and they will occasionally rub their arms for warmth.

Crossed Arms– In general, this gesture may indicate defensiveness. Now, this does not mean the person is purposely sitting there thinking, "I don't want to hear what you have to say. I am shutting you out." What it does mean is that the person will filter everything they hear through how it affects them. Gerald I. Nierenberger, author of *How to Read a Person Like a Book,* studied over two thousand negotiations and found that not one closed when the participants' arms and legs were crossed. Before any negotiation closed each party uncrossed their arms and legs and moved to an open position.

Contracted Pupils– Ever heard the terms "beady little eyes" or "snake eyes"? Contracted pupils are seen as dishonest or angry and withholding of information. When people become very upset, they tend to squint their eyes and purse their mouths. Contracted pupils, when coupled with rolling of the eyes, is an expression of disgust. Because of the negative associations that come with squinting or contracted pupils, try to choose seating away from direct sunlight so you keep an open look to your face.

Hand Supporting the Chin– This gesture shows boredom. You literally could knock the hand away and the face would fall flat on the table. It appears as if the person has no interest in what you are

saying. This gesture, combined with glazed eyes and vacant nods, means you have lost your audience. If you get this gesture a lot, it may mean you are giving too many details and your listener has tuned out. Try stating your point first and then giving the supporting data. If you want to test whether this sign signals that you have given too many details and have lost the person, just stop talking. The person will usually jump in and move on to something else. You will also get this gesture if you spend too much time talking about you and not the other person. Negative people will often use this bored gesture.

Hands Clenched Together– This gesture is a sign that the person is frustrated. The higher the hands go, the more frustrated the person

is. Stop talking and ask questions. Ask, "What are your thoughts on this?" "Do you agree with that statement?" "What ideas do you have?" or "What challenges do you think we face with this new idea?" You can bet the person has some ideas.

If you don't address objections right there, people will tend to retain the negativity and tell everyone else why they disagree but you will never know. Do not try to close a deal when you see this gesture. Instead, find out what they are upset about. They might disagree with a state-

ment you made or they might feel you are talking over them. Ask questions to get them involved. Children will use this gesture with their parents while they are being disciplined. Children know they cannot talk back, so they express their frustration with this gesture.

Tip: Notice that all questions asked are open-ended rather than yes/no questions. This gets the other party more involved in your discussion, presentation or negotiation.

Picking at Imaginary Lint– This is my personal favorite. According to Alan Pease, this means the person disapproves of the opinion or idea stated but feels constrained in offering an opinion. You definitely want to ask for input here.

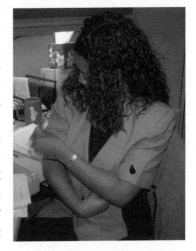

Stop and ask for their thoughts and opinions. One on one acknowledge that you sense unease and ask why. In a group situation, it's best to wait until you can do this privately with the individual. Ask if there are any issues or points they'd like to clarify. This allows the other person expression and input without having to talk in front of the entire group. Remember picking imaginary lint signals a feeling of constraint in offering up one's thoughts or opinions.

You will often see this gesture when in response to an inappropriate joke. Whatever you do, do not ignore this gesture! You run the risk of making people feel like you don't care what they think. If you talk with them privately and take action on what they say, it shows sensitivity and reinforces their confidence that they can come to you with any issues or problems.

Deceit Signs

Take these signs with a grain of salt. You want to watch the gestures that accompany these signs or you will erroneously assume that everyone who scratches their nose is lying to you.

If someone uses these gestures while talking to you, it may indicate lying or withholding of information. If they do these gestures while you are talking to them, it may indicate they are skeptical of what you are saying. Either way, these are important gestures to watch for.

If they are deceit signs, generally you will see the gestures accompanied by some of the following: squirming, breaking eye contact, shifting of eyes, shifting of body, turning the body away from you, voice level rising in volume and pitch.

In a negotiation this lets you know whether they are serious about the offer you are making or if they are going to just keep pressing you to give in more.

Eye Rub– According to Desmond Morris, if it is a big lie, a woman will rub lightly and look at the ceiling. A man will rub vigorously and look at the floor. Either way, the gesture is intended to avoid eye contact with the other person.

Nose Touching– Look for a slow rub by one finger just under the nose. This can be distinguished from allergies or general itchiness which is usually alleviated by hard rubbing on the top of the nose.

Ear Rub– This may be a finger behind the ear, in the ear, or rubbing the back of the ear. This is another way of avoiding eye contact. It is the brain's attempt to replace eye contact with a distracting activity.

Collar Pull– According to Desmond Morris, this gesture signifies that the person suspects they will be caught. They don't think you will really buy into their lie. Ever heard the term, "feeling the noose tightening"?

When a person lies there is a definite chemical reaction within the body. Blood vessels will swell, body temperature will go up and there will be a sense of discomfort. Because of this, a person will pull at their collar to relieve the tension.

Neck Scratch– At the same time all of these chemical reactions happen in your body, a tingling sensation may pass up the spine. Desmond Morris found a person will scratch exactly five times to relieve the itch.

Such gestures can be used for decent motives as well as dishonorable ones. Especially since we can't always say exactly what we are

thinking. Think about the last time a friend asked you if you liked her new outfit, and you thought it was hideous. Maybe you said "Oh, where did you get it? It really is you!" At the same time you probably unconsciously employed one of these deceit gestures which betrayed your true opinion.

Body Language Fluency And Outcome Thinking™

How does body language work with Outcome Thinking™? Well, remember the basic goal of Outcome Thinking™ is to achieve positive results without conflict, and the key to this is communication. Body language skills can assist us in both sending and receiving accurate messages. You want to use positive body language when you communicate with other people. You need to make sure you make good eye contact, smile, tilt your head, and give reassuring gestures such as nodding your head. Most importantly, make sure your body language matches your message. If it doesn't, people will instinctively rely on your body language more than your words. At best, you will leave them very confused as to what your real message was.

Read Them Like A Book

As a teenager getting ready for dates, I would spend hours creating what I thought was a casual, pulled together look. Sometimes I would come downstairs and my Mom would look over her reading glasses, look me up and down and say, "Is *that* what you're wearing?" Of course, I would immediately bristle. "Yes, why? What's wrong with it?" She would resume her reading and say, "Nothing, I was just wondering."

Right.

We've all had the experience where the words didn't match the total message. I knew from her tone of voice and her body language that she disapproved. As a teenager, I would prod for her to tell me the truth—she hated my outfit. As adults, we often simply let it go, while harboring resentment at the lack of candor.

Well, people you work with react the same way. If you are the boss, people are especially sensitive to what you are saying and thinking about them. Your staff spends a lot of time trying to decipher *you instead* of focusing on *the job*. This is why I always recommend that you sit down with each person and tell them exactly how you like to work. Then ask them what are their pet peeves and how they like to work. This makes your people feel like you believe in them and respect them. It also helps you respect your people if you do know the little things that irritate them.

I personally have a few quirks. One of them is that I love pens and will only write with certain pens. I can't stand it if someone takes a pen off my desk. Other quirks are that when I am out of the office, I want my mail arranged from urgent to not important. That way when I get back I can sail through the most important things and get to the other stuff at leisure.

I also don't take criticism personally. I feel like I constantly need to improve so I am always looking for my team to tell me what I need to work on. I don't take offense to it.

I also will sometimes recognize a trait in myself, but will be okay with it. For example, I tend to get excited about new projects and get many ideas at one time. This can drive my team nuts because they feel like I am going in so many different directions. I love this creativity in me and don't want to change it. Instead I asked my team to stop me when they need to know what is to be of focus right now so there is no confusion.

I have found that by sitting down with each person there is very little tension when problems come up. Each person knows where the other person stands so we spend the time on the issue at hand rather than the emotions. For example, I tell everyone that I don't care about mistakes since they mean we are growing and learning. I do care that we learn from all mistakes, admit to them and look for solutions. I tell them that I can't stand when people try to defend or justify a mistake, just say what you want to do to correct it. I also tell them that I only hired them because I believe in them and that no mistake will make me not trust them but hiding it or being defensive about it will. I will always go over what happened and how to avoid it in the future. If it is an issue with a customer, I always take the responsibility of the decision so my team doesn't feel targeted.

This has lead to more direct conversation in my office regarding mistakes and problems that arise. People let go of defending why it happened and just look for the solution. They no longer wonder what I think of them, but instead trust their own instincts.

I have also used this method when it comes to making decisions. I tell my team I would rather have them make a decision and have it be wrong then to look to me to have all the answers. I tell them I will support them in their decision and then we will go over a better way to handle it in the future. All I ask is that they are open to learning.

If you share a cube with another person or you have people that work under you, I highly recommend that you sit down with each person and go over how to work best with each other. You will probably find that little things really can throw a person off.

Space

Space is a form of body language; it's our comfort zone, it can affect how we perceive others. I worked with one woman who felt that co-workers didn't respect her. She complained that people would use her phone and put the receiver down backwards, and that they would use her stapler and leave it turned out away from her. When pressed she pointed to these two little things as the reasons why she felt people didn't respect her. She equated her space with herself.

Space is very important to pay attention to if you want someone to be receptive to your message. When you stand too close to a person there's a tendency to step away from you. The focus becomes regaining body space back and not your message.

TAKE ACTION

To find what your space distance is, start watching your-self after you shake a person's hand. What distance do you try to keep between you? Do you put weight on your back foot to get a little better spacing or do you lean into the person? On average, most people like two to four feet of space when talking business. With friends and family, we general-ly like one to two feet. Our intimate space zone is zero to ten inches. This is called our "bubble space."

I recommend that you think about the *result* you want from each encounter with a person and adapt accordingly. For example, if you are with a client and the client has a small bubble space and you have a large bubble space, you would try to make the client comfortable. You would stand still while the client leans in. You wouldn't try to back away. If you do back away, the other person may feel you can't relate to them or that you don't like them.

On the flip side, if you have a small space and your client has a large space, you might be invading their space. If you find people stepping back from you, leaning to one side or shuffling their feet, you may be standing too close. When you are too close to some-one, they will feel that you are suffocating them and that you are not very considerate. Worse, they could feel threatened, particularly in opposite sex situations.

I have seen this one habit kill some people's career. Usually people who invade other people's body space also talk incessantly. Remember, when you over-talk and tell too many details, people will have a tendency to tune you out. In my experience, very few people that have these tendencies move up to be top management. The few that do are often left out of the loop when new informa-tion comes down because people don't want to deal with all of the details.

TAKE ACTION: Practicing Reading Body Language

As with any other language, speaking and reading body language comes with practice. I recommend that you try some of the following:

1. Watch cartoons. Cartoons are great because we are not influenced by appearance. We draw our conclusions as to the emotions of inanimate cartoon objects solely from their "body language." Take the magic carpet in "Aladdin." When we first met the carpet it showed fear (by timidly walking forward on its tassels and hiding), anxiety (by shakily peeking a tassel out), desire for friendship (by extending a tassel for a handshake), rejection (by dragging its tassels as it slowly slumps away), and excitement (by stretching out and shaking its tassels). All its emotions are human characteristics shown through body language.

   Try turning off the volume and see if you can discern the emotions and thoughts of the characters.

2. Rent any Disney film. Look for the reactions on the faces and bodies of the animated characters. Some great films for this include: "Aladdin," "Beauty and the Beast," "Little Mermaid," and "101 Dalmatians." Write down the emotions you see. Stop and review to see if you missed any. Then write down which gestures and postures are associated with those emotions.

   Or, watch any film for five minutes without the sound. Rewind and see if you understood what was going on by reading the body language.

3. Try to read others and restate the emotion you thought you read in their body language. For example, if you are talking with someone and you see an expression of what you think is confusion, stop and ask if what you just said made sense. Make sure you understand the emotion you read on their face. Please, do *not* try to tell the person what they are feeling or thinking. This will tick a person off.

I Didn't Mean To Cross My Legs In That Tone Of Voice

One word of caution: Sometimes a person's face may reflect an emotion that has nothing to do with you. For example, let's say you are meeting with someone and right away the person is brisk, drums his fingers and looks away. You think he is bored so you rush through your meeting. The reality might be that a crisis erupted right before you arrived and his mind is absorbed with how he is going to handle it.

Consequently, it is best to vocalize what you think you see to determine if you are accurate. In this case you might say, "I really respect your time and I sense that even though we set this appointment up, it might not be the best time for you right now. Do you still want to meet or would you like to set up another time?" The person then must choose to either give you his attention and set aside the other issue, or admit he prefers to meet at another time. Either way it's a better scenario. He will appreciate you sensed his edginess and you will have a more productive meeting.

4. Enlist people's help in monitoring your own body language. Ask them to point out negative signals you maybe unaware of. Try not to be defensive. Once you have determined what signals you want to change, appoint someone to alert you every time you perform that gesture. Many of our gestures arise from the subconscious level, and we need to bring them up to the conscious level before we can change them.

I have worked with many people who use body signs they are completely unaware of. One man would lick his lips when a difficult question was asked. Another woman rolled her eyes under pressure. Some tapped their feet or slouched in their seat. In negotiations, negative body signs can stop the entire negotiation.

Early in my career, I had someone come in to observe me during negotiations because I noticed that at a certain point they either closed or fell apart. This would occur right after we had agreed on a couple of options and were just tightening up what we wanted to do. To my horror, the observer reported that, unbeknownst to me, I was engaged in self-sabotaging body language. He told me when the other person repeated what we said, or asked a question I thought was lame I would get a look on my face that said, "What language do you want me to say it in? Didn't you get it?" This look put people on the defense and the negotiations went downhill from there. Of course, that's not the message I wanted to send at all, and I felt badly that I was inadvertently signaling condescension.

Once I figured out what body language I was using that threw things off, I had to work to change it. I did that by having an ally sit in each session, facing me. He would scratch his nose anytime he saw me making the gesture. This allowed me to catch it in time, look away, check my emotions and change my thoughts.

Remember that your body language reflects your thoughts so you have to work at changing your thoughts as well.

> 5. Role-play with someone. Just take any upcoming interaction and enlist a friend to play the role of the other person. This will give you practice with your body language in tandem with Outcome Thinking™. Then discuss what you each thought and felt during the role-play. I recommend you videotape it.

I chuckle when a manager tells me to video tape all his employees, but then refuses to participate himself, thinking there is nothing for him to learn. It is unbelievable how many signs people give off and never realize it. Once these managers see themselves on tape, they are amazed. They often find they twitch, tap toes, slouch or do any number of body signs they were unaware of! So, I highly recommend that even seasoned people tape themselves to catch any nuances.

> 6. People-watch. Go out to a busy restaurant with a friend and try to read the conversations that are going on around you. What person is bored? Interested? Who is married, who's dating? Who are friends? Co-workers? Employee and employer? What signs tell you these things? Who is upset? Indifferent? Make a game of it and just enjoy yourself.

Be A Mind Reader

Remember that reading body language effectively takes years of practice. At first you will be so aware of the body language that you may focus totally on that and miss some of the words. Keep practicing until it comes easily. One thing you will find as you become more adept at reading body language is that people will say you are so intuitive. They will feel like you can read their mind when actually they themselves are clearly telling you what they are thinking and feeling.

....

Voicing the Message

Outcome Thinking™: Choosing The Right Words
....
Phrasing For Success

Our next step is becoming conscious of the words you choose to use when communicating. When talking with a person, we tend to slip into dialogue that reflects our true thoughts. For example, let's say you are meeting with a group and you feel that one person is dominating. You feel that everything on the table is really only one person's input. You want everyone to feel a part of the process; so you might say, "Let's just get rid of all of this crap and start with a fresh slate." Ouch! The word "crap" instead of "stuff" slipped out because, in your mind, you don't think the ideas are worthwhile. Like body language our actual words can reveal our true thoughts.

Outcome Thinking™ requires on-the-spot analysis of the best way to phrase things to get the best results. Using the previous scenario, a better approach would be to say, "I really want everyone to participate in the results here. We've had some great input from Pat and I really appreciate the participation—now it's time to hear from the rest of you. So let's table what we have and move to some more ideas. Jill, what are your thoughts?"

What Does This Mean To "We"?
....
Outcome Thinking™ requires *that you assume full responsibility for whether the other person understood your message or not.* This means that *you follow through* to make sure things get done. This creates a WE thinking process instead of a ME thinking process. I

111

will admit that this can be frustrating at first, especially if you work with people who like to push things off onto others.

What you will find if you use this communication, is that people take more ownership and more responsibility for how they communicate. Remember, what motivates others to action is in direct proportion to their perception of its personal relevance. If you really need information from another person try to think how you can make it personally relevant, so they want to get you the information.

Framing The Message

Speak Clearly On Paper Too

I worked with one insurance company that had to get some critical information from their clients in order to process their paperwork. They would send a letter stating all the things they needed along with why they needed them. They really spent a great deal of time putting together this well-written letter. Still, they did not get the information back that they requested. Even phone calls were ignored.

Now, how would we approach this problem with Outcome Thinking™? You would step back and ask yourself, "What is the result I need?"—to get the information back so I can process their insurance in a timely fashion and "how can I make it easy for them to do this?"

For starters, we changed the letter so the first line read,

"In order to get your insurance processed, the following items are needed:

☐ *Physical exam by doctor*
☐ *Medical history transferred over*
☐ *Results from blood test*

If we do not receive these items by _____(insert date), we will be unable to process your insurance. Please call (phone number here) to verify we have received all of your items."

After this, they could then explain why they needed each of the items.

Never assume people read everything you write. Always highlight the information that you need them to notice and put it in bite size chunks that they can quickly react to. Even when you do this, you might not get the response you want. Keep working on it until you do.

The second thing we did was analyze all the messages the claims adjusters were leaving for the policy holders. Most left a message something like this, "This is Susan Johnson from KPT Company calling. We have not received your paperwork to file your insurance. Please give me a call at..." Once you have left a few such messages you can begin to feel like a pest. On top of that, because the message was not compelling, people become immune after a while.

So we changed the message to say, "Hi. This is Susan Johnson calling from KPT Company. In order to complete your insurance request we need to get the following from you: (list items). Please call me by tomorrow at (phone number) to let me know where we stand. *I want to make sure your insurance doesn't lapse.* If I don't hear from you tomorrow, I will try to reach you at this number again." Note the line about "your insurance" lapsing. Aha! Now there's a personal stake for the insurance holder.

This phone call, along with the changes in the letter, brought about better results. Remember, most people aren't *trying* to make your life more difficult. They just don't see how the information you need from them is very important to them personally. It is your job to help them understand why you are requesting certain things. If they perceive your request merely as something that *you* want, you will never be at the top of their to-do list.

Minimize Distracting Messages

In the speaking industry, I travel a lot and am often on the road. From years of experience I know that if the little details are not taken care of people will focus entirely on that and miss the message. I once did a program on Outcome Thinking™ for five hundred people and the room was just charged with enthusiasm. It was one of those events that left me excited and energized. The client company had expected about three hundred people for the event, so they were overwhelmed by the positive response, and a bit unprepared. This meant that their quantities of juice, coffee and cookies were way off and they soon ran out.

At the end of the session, several people came up to talk about how to use their new skills in situations that they personally faced. One man, however, stepped forward to tell me how he resented that I didn't care more for my audience, that I was too cheap to buy enough cookies and juice and that I just made sure I had enough water up front for me. Guess he missed the entire point of Outcome Thinking™!

I was absolutely blown away. He deprived himself of any benefit from the session because he focused on the insufficient cookies. He assumed I had ordered the cookies and was too cheap to buy enough. He never attempted to look at the situation from a positive angle or to imagine alternative explanations.

Because it is so important to me that my audience focuses on the message being delivered during a program, I have created a Preparation Sheet that tells people exactly what they need to have at each session and why. We have a room set-up sheet that shows exactly how the room should be set up. The person planning the meeting can just fax the room set-up to the hotel, and all details will be taken care of. Then we call two days prior to quick-check that all the details from the Preparation Sheet have been addressed and to confirm any new developments.

One of the things on the Preparation Sheet says:

Name Tags: Please have name tags for all attendees to put their first name on. Since our programs are highly interactive, this helps me develop a rapport with the audience. Please provide large black markers for people to write on their name tags.

Even with that right on the sheet about 70% of the time people either don't have name tags or do have name tags but only have pencils or pens for people to write on them. Well, from the front of a room you can't read a name tag that is written in pencil or pen.

We are still puzzled as to what to do to make sure this is covered. It might mean bringing name tags, changing where we have them placed on the Preparation Sheet or just bringing large black markers. I don't know the answer yet, but I do know it is my responsibility and not my clients. Many of these people only plan a couple of meetings a year so they don't see the importance of such a small item. Yet it can make a big difference in the synergy of the room.

Keep it Simple And Direct

In your communication with others, keep things simple. If you need information at a certain time, convey the consequences and the reasons for them if you don't have it on time. Assume people want to do what's best and that they probably are just not aware of what complications they are causing.

This is a tricky piece. If you don't assume the best of the other person, you can assume a very condescending, take charge, snotty or rigid tone to your message. And you don't want that.

I recently got some new marketing materials put together. I needed to make some changes to the copy so I thought I would be helpful and type the changes on to disk rather than mark up the paper copy. Well, when I met with the designer she explained that it is a lot more work for them to take my disk and format it. She said it would be a lot easier for them if I just wrote the changes on the paper and faxed them in.

I am sure I frustrated her by having all this information on the disk. She told me that many clients do that. Do you hear comments like that from your clients? That is your red flag that you aren't communicating clearly enough. In this case, a great idea would be to fax the copy along with a note that says, "Please only make written changes to the hard copy. If you retype on to a disk, your project will be delayed since we will have to reformat everything. Don't worry about the copy getting too messy for us to read."

Look at your area at work. Are there places where you can be more direct with your communication with people?

Perception Words

Just exactly what does that mean?

Perception words are words that you personally assign a meaning to based on your experience. I find that most miscommunication comes from perception words. To test this ask a few co-workers to write down their responses to the following questions, but not to say anything out loud.

1. My neighbor bought a very expensive car. How much did it cost?

2. Someone tells you they work for an older boss. How old is the boss?

3. A person tells you they will get back to you in the near future. When are they getting back to you?

4. Someone tells you they stood in a really long line. How many people were in line?

Now compare all the answers and note the high and low of the group. I do this with groups all over the country and the responses I get always vary from one end of the spectrum to the other.

"Expensive car" generally spans from $20K to $100K, "older boss" ranges from forty years to sixty-five years. "Near future" could mean anything from fifteen minutes to never, and "long line" reaches from three to two hundred people.

Everyone based their answers on some experience in their life or an experience from someone they know. That is their reality base for their expectations. Any time you don't meet people's expectations, they will feel you have failed them. This is why it is so important to avoid using perception words if you can.

Common Perception Words

Never	Frequently	Most of the time
Always	Rarely	Occasionally
Often	Usually	In a short while
Seldom	Quite often	Soon
Almost always	A lot	Shortly
Possibly	Probably	

These words conjure up different images in each person's mind. You might tell someone that you will get back to them shortly. To you, it might mean tomorrow and to them it might mean in thirty minutes. Now, when you don't call back in thirty minutes, they will begin to think you are not reliable.

Misunderstanding Or Misperception?

I have a girl friend that will rarely directly commit to attending an event. Instead she will say, "I probably will go." Well, for me "probably" means I am 70% sure I will go since I think "probably" gets a person's hopes up. To my friend, "probably" means she's only 30% sure she will go. I used to get upset when I planned things and she didn't show up. I felt I couldn't rely on her. After a while, whenever she said "probably," I asked what that meant on a scale of 1-10 with 10 being "Yes, I'll be there."

The funny thing is that if she had just said "no," or "I'm not sure, so don't count me in." I wouldn't have been upset. What upset me was the expectation that she would "probably" show up. Now in this scenario, clearly no one is right and no one is wrong. What we have here are simply two different interpretations of what the word "probably" means. Fortunately we recognized this before it exploded into hurt feelings and further miscommunication. *HOT TIP: Whenever you are negotiating or trying to get a decision on something ask "On a scale of 1-10, where would you say we are with implementing _____?"*

Clear Speaking For Clear Results

Look at your own communication at work. How can you make it clearer? What about in your personal life? Do you have a hard time saying "no"? Many people that have a hard time saying "no" will instead give a vague answer, feeling that is the "nice" way to let a person down. In fact, people handle concrete answers better than vague answers. People can better deal with a simple "yes" or "no" instead of a "possibly."

Another way we invite misunderstanding is by not providing enough information as to our expectations. When we leave voice messages we sometimes say, "This is Anne Warfield from IMP calling. Please give me a call at 888-IMP-9421." You have provided no indication as to the importance of the call or when you'll be available.

Instead say, "This is Anne Warfield from IMP calling. Please give me a call at 888-IMP-9421. I will be in the office today until 5 PM, tomorrow from 11 AM to 4 PM and Wednesday all day." This helps eliminate phone tag since the person knows exactly when to get you. It also puts more of the responsibility on them to get back to you because you have left the times that you can be reached. Moreover, it creates the impression that this is not simply a casual request. If, in fact, you are just calling to chat, say so. "Hi, call me at your leisure...just wanted to catch up on a few things."

Outcome Thinking™ results in having each person become more accountable and more WE oriented. How? Because if you hold each person accountable for the delivery of the message, then no one can make excuses or shift the blame. As a manager, it allows you to be much more direct with your people while boosting morale.

Let's say you have an employee who is continually late. Typically, you might say, "You are late again. Next time I'll write you up," or "Part of the requirements of this job is to be on time. I can't have you come in late anymore." Or you ask why they are late and you then have to deal with a ton of excuses.

With Outcome Thinking™, focus on the result you want: for the person to be on time. Think positively from their perspective; perhaps they don't pay much attention to time, they don't realize how it throws the entire team off when they are late and assume positively that they want to do a good job. Now you would approach them and say, "Tom, I know you are conscientious about your job. An important aspect of your job is to be here at 8:00 a.m. and that is not happening. What needs to be done in order for you to get here at eight every morning?"

This then leads to a discussion. Tom may never have considered alternatives to his morning routine. Once he's told you what he is going to do to be on time, then you would wrap up the conversation. "Okay. So from now on I can expect you here by 8 a.m. since you will have a new alarm clock? Great."

If, for some reason, he still comes late, you can then approach him with direct consequences. For example, "Tom, we both agreed that you would be here by 8 AM every day and you were still late twice this last week. Since being late is not acceptable, what would you do if you were me?" You will often find that people will be a lot harder on themselves than you would be.

Negative Words Breed Negative Reactions

Two perfectly good words you'll want to use sparingly are "But" and "However." Why? Because "But" and "However" tend to negate whatever you just said, and cause the focus to shift to the last part of your statement. Consequently, someone may over-emphasize that portion of your comment and perceive it out of proportion. For example, you say, "Tom you are a really good worker, but you always miss deadlines." This causes the person to focus on missed deadlines and to feel you are criticizing. Instead say, "Tom, you are a really good worker and you always miss deadlines. Deadlines may not be missed. What do you need from me in order to meet all deadlines?" Once they tell you what they need and it is agreed to, stick to it. The first time something is missed remind them of the agreement.

Okay, you might be shaking your head here saying "No way, Anne. I am not laying the blame on me by saying 'What do you need from me in order to meet all deadlines!' That will just make me the scapegoat."

I'll admit it sounds like that is what you are doing. In reality because you are willing to take ownership for what you can change, the other person feels obligated to take ownership for their part. It also allows you to learn if there are things you are doing that might be inhibiting others.

In a *Wall Street Journal* study, people said they felt more comfortable when they had more responsibility and control at work. People actually do want to assume responsibility. So look at ways you can do this. Explore ways you yourself can assume more responsibility in your own job. There is a lot more pride when there is a lot more freedom.

Be Positively Effective

As you can see, with Outcome Thinking™ you are always coming from the positive angle. You realize that what you know is limited and you do not assume you know "why" someone did or said something. Most miscommunication comes from misinterpreting what a person meant.

Are You Positively Clear On That?

Remember that you may not have all the information necessary to make a decision. A small bit of information can change the whole way you think about something. Consider this true story:

There is a large crowd waiting at a train depot in New York. It is a cold and blustery day and people are pushing and shoving to get on the train. On the platform is Edwin, a well known actor and Robert, a prominent politician's son. As the people are pushing and shoving, Robert falls off the platform. Edwin notices and yells up to the conductor to stop the train. But the conductor can't hear over all the noise, so Edwin reaches down, grabs Robert and pulls him to safety. In that split second their lives crossed: Edwin Boothe and Robert Todd Lincoln. Just a few years later their two families would meet again, when Edwin's brother, John Wilkes Boothe would shoot and kill Abraham Lincoln, Robert's father.

Now, doesn't that bit of information change how you look at history? Don't you wonder if Abraham Lincoln got to know Edward and perhaps helped his career? Did Robert and Edward become friends? Was John Wilkes Boothe jealous of his brother? Is that why he shot Abraham Lincoln in a theater? Was Edward on stage that night? This one story gives a whole new slant to a prominent part of our history. So never assume you know the whole story.

Repeat After Me...

With Outcome Thinking™, repeat back what you heard the other person say. Why? Because as you listen to a person, you filter their words through your experiences and that skews what you hear. You might attach a completely different interpretation to a person's words than they intended. Repeating what you heard is especially helpful in dealing with customer complaints. In order to get to the results you both want, you must be clear on what they are. You must be on the same wave length as to precisely what "satisfaction" means, or you run the risk of losing a client and gaining a bad-willed ambassador who will share the negative experience with others.

PART FOUR

Outcome Thinking™ Results in Sales

Sales

Outcome Thinking™ is a great life skill, especially when negotiating or giving sales presentations. It's natural to negotiate and sell by thinking, "What would I want to hear?" Not a bad approach, but very limiting. Not all customers are motivated by the same things you are. The features of a product you think are the greatest might be the ones they like the least. On top of that, everyone wants to feel unique and special. They want to know that you customized your presentation just for them.

Mentally picture that you are going to add value to every person you meet, and you will automatically start thinking from that person's angle. Most deals are lost because the salesperson just answers questions without thinking of *why* the person is asking the question.

So You Think You Know What They Want...

For example, imagine that you work in the trust department of a bank. Sally comes in to see you about her parents' estate. You are walking her through the reasons why your bank should handle the trust. Sally asks, "Does the person named as executor of the estate always remain the same? Can my parents come in any time they want and get things changed?" You feel confident because easy access is one of your bank's strong suits. You respond, "The executor can be changed and absolutely your parents may come in anytime. We actually encourage it so they feel comfortable with us." Sally leaves and you lose the sale. Why?

Sally asked the question because her Mother has Alzheimer's

disease and her Dad has difficulty controlling her. Sally is concerned how such easy access would compromise the whole point of having an executor. What if her parents come in, without one of the children, and just change everything? She wants to feel secure that you wouldn't just let them change things without safeguards.

It would have been best to ask Sally a few questions. "Are you looking for an account that is easily accessible by your parents?" She would have then explained that she wanted to have the account protected and why. That would have allowed you to explain how you protect an account. Always clarify the true nature of the question they want answered.

Do You Want A Sale Or A Soapbox?

Stop trying to sell from your perspective. Remember your assumptions are based on your experience and no one person's experience matches your own. You are there to learn where your client has come from, where they are going, and how you can help them get there.

Once you address their needs and desires, price will no longer be an objection. If you do get a lot of objections about price, it means you are not doing enough up front to create value to the client. Remember there is a market for Lexus and there is a market for Hyundai. If you are selling Lexus then you need to make the customer picture that.

Buyers Buy Benefits

A great technique to help you with objections is to create what I call a "benefit sheet." A benefit sheet tells people clearly why they should use you. It is written in simple language that they can use to tell others *why* they used you. Point out even the things that seem obvious to you. They may not be obvious to others. Do you know all the steps in an oil change?

Jiffy Lube did a great job capitalizing on this, and became known as the expert in oil changes. They simply told the public that they do a ten point oil change and then described all of the ten points. Well, let's face it, an oil change is just an oil change. This was a great strategy because it was the first time anyone spelled out clearly what was done in an oil change. During the oil change itself, they even yell out what they are doing while you are in the waiting room so you know each point is covered. Just knowing the information gives people the confidence that they are making the right choice in choosing Jiffy Lube.

Why You?

Think about all the reasons a person should do business with you. Look at your company's years of experience, your years of experience and anything else that sets your company apart. Think of common objections you hear and then turn them into benefits of doing business with you. For example, let's say you get a lot of objections to your pricing. In your benefit sheet you might have "Top Quality. Our customers use us because we have the best quality in the industry. Our price reflects our commitment to you to keep investing in new technologies and staying leaders in our industry." This statement reassures clients that your price reflects quality and new technology. Remember people are willing to pay, if they think the value is in the price.

The Benefit Sheet: Checklist For The Good Stuff

What To Include And Why

Here is a sample of some items from our benefit sheet:

Customization

All keynotes and programs are customized to meet your needs and objectives. You have unique challenges and frustrations your people face in their jobs. Anne builds a message that provides your people with the skills they need to tackle these challenges and frustrations. For each hour Anne speaks to your organization, she puts in about ten hours of time in research.

Satisfaction Guarantee

Anne is ranked at a 9.04 on a scale of 1-10 by her audiences. That is a cumulative ranking from 1991 to the present!

Creates A "WE" Atmosphere

Think how well your company would run if everyone felt a sense of ownership and accountability. Anne helps people take ownership for how they are perceived, how they want to be perceived and what they need to do to build rapport with others.

The benefit sheet goes on to list eight key points that set IMP apart from other businesses. They are all written from the customer's viewpoint and all show how they benefit the customer.

To begin your benefit sheet, I recommend you list why a customer should buy from you. What is special about your product? About you? About your company? Just list all of the items.

For example, let's imagine you work for an insurance company. Here is how your list might look:

- Company has been around 70 years.
- I have been an agent for 5 years.
- We give 5% of our money back to the community.
- We offer all areas of insurance-health, life, home and auto.
- We are financially stable.
- Flexible.
- We give great customer service.

Next, you would compose a key phrase to support each item and show it as a benefit. So here is how your benefit sheet might look at this stage:

Benefits Unique To XYZ Insurance

At XYZ Insurance, we strive to provide you with the best insurance in the industry. Some unique benefits to our company include:

Focused Customer Service

At XYZ Insurance, we don't just sell you a policy. We are committed to helping you have the right policy at the right time for you. We know the real crunch comes when you need a claim handled. That is why we have agents personally handle all claims under $_____. We work fast for you!

Dependable

You can depend on us to be there for you. We have an A+ rating. What this means for you is we are financially stable, and we're going to be here when you need us.

Progressive

Just as your lifestyle changes, we change to fit the times. We know you would rather never have a catastrophe. Therefore, we invest in creating programs that can help reduce the difficulties in the aftermath of a catastrophe.

Experienced

Navigating the world of insurance can be frustrating and intimidating. I work with you to make sure you get what's right for you. I draw on my five years experience to help you.

Best Value

We are committed to giving you the best service and insurance for the value. We will never compromise value for price.

Flexible

We understand that your life is hectic so we work with your schedule, not ours.

The benefit sheet helps people focus on why they should work with you. A brochure is beautiful, but most people will not read it. And when they sit down and compare products they will have often forgotten most of what you said. Put it in writing. Make it simple for them.

If you would like some samples of benefit sheets, please call, fax or e-mail our office. All of our numbers are at the back of the book. We'd also love to see what creative and compelling benefit sheets you come up with after reading this book!

Even if you don't give the benefit sheet to a client, it helps you clarify your strengths so you can better answer objections. It works—I've seen it work for many companies, and it will work for you too!

PART FIVE

Real-Life
Applications of
Outcome Thinking™

Get Real

Now you try it.

The following is a format I recommend you use to think through each situation clearly before you respond.

Situation:

Here you list what is the situation you face.

Result/outcome desired:

What result do you want?

Other person's perspective:

Here you list what the other person's perspective might be, *thinking only from the positive perspective!* If you have problems with this, have someone try to help you with it. Think not only of their perspective on this issue, but delve deeper into discovering their inner goals and desires. The more you can tie into what their true desires might be, the better you will be at connecting with them.

Think in terms of the following graph:

Their Perspective
on the issue

Their Inner Core
goals &
desires

Best way to phrase it:

Make sure you do not use "but" or "however." Make sure you keep it positive. Make sure your phrase takes into account the other person's good intentions. Watch out for words that can be seen as negative.

Here's The Situation...

The following are real situations when people wanted to know how to use Outcome Thinking™ to resolve conflict. Read through each situation and first see how you would handle it. Then read the Outcome Thinking™ answer. Remember, each example offers just one possible way to handle the situation. You may come up with other ways that you feel are even better!

Note that the areas are divided into categories—Dealing with your boss and co-workers, with employees, with customers, and with friends and family. You can focus on areas that interest you most. These are real scenarios provided by real people, along with the solutions we applied. You may not agree with all of them. That's okay! Remember to maintain your own distinct style while applying Outcome Thinking™.

If you have a particular situation to which you would like to apply Outcome Thinking™, you are invited to phone, fax or e-mail us. The numbers are all located at the back of your book.

In The Workplace: Bosses And Co-Workers
· ·

Situation:
You are feeling overwhelmed with projects. You are not sure what is most important at this moment. Just then, your boss walks by and asks you to please type up notes from a just concluded meeting. How do you handle this?

Outcome desired:
You want to keep peace with your boss and still have him/her understand your workload.

Other person's view:
Your boss probably does not realize how many projects you are working on. Your boss wants the area to look good and wants a good job done.

Best phrased:
"Bob, I would love to type up your notes from your meeting. My concern is getting them back to you in a timely fashion. I am currently juggling several projects, so I need to know if you are okay with getting the notes back next Friday. Or would you like to look over what I am working on and see if we need to reprioritize things? Or perhaps you can enlist someone else to do them right now."

This lets your boss know you respect him and that you want to do a good job. It also keeps you from getting stressed out by having to decide what projects to delay. Many bosses forget what projects they have given you so they are not aware of everything you are juggling.

Situation:

You hear rumors about some upcoming changes that will take place at the company. You are wondering how they will affect your job. How do you handle this?

Outcome desired:

You want to know that you have job security and to operate from facts instead of gossip.

Other person's view:

(This varies according to your position and the position of the person you are talking with. In this scenario we will assume you talk to your boss.)

Your boss wants to have a work environment that is productive and not stressful. If the rumor involves a buyout or merger, they may not legally talk about it until it is signed. So they may want to give information, but are unable. Your boss may also be in the dark on what is going on.

Best phrased:

"I just heard about some possible changes in the company. I knew you would be direct with me, so I thought I would stop in and see if you had heard anything about...." OR "Have you heard anything about the possible changes in the company and what effects they might have on different positions?"

Resist the temptation to assume that your boss is trying to withhold information. If you do assume that, you will come off as defensive rather than legitimately curious.

Situation:

Your company is expanding. You are feeling lost in the shuffle. It seems people are packing offices and moving to new space almost daily. You know your area will be moved next but you don't know where it will be moved. How do you handle this?

Outcome desired:

You want the warm atmosphere and security of knowing that some things are stable. Also you want to be relaxed and not stressed through the move. You want to know that you can look forward to the change, and that you'll love your new office.

Other person's view:

They are trying to adapt and are probably frustrated with the moves as well. They are trying to do the best job possible. They might not realize how stressful the move is to you and others.

Best phrased:

"Betty, I was wondering if you could just take a second to talk with me about when our move will take place and where we'll be moving to? I really want to focus on my work at hand and would like to be able to plan for the move." Once she gives you the information on the move you may want to say, "I know we are growing and expanding and everyone is coping as best we can. Moving can be stressful. Maybe we need a mental-health break—can we look at some ways of releasing the stress?"

Then be prepared to offer some ideas such as a quick party, posting of the new offices, new area quick tours, 5-minute stress releasers, etc. Make it fun and productive rather than torture.

Situation:

You and several other people report directly to Keith and Sheila. You actually directly support Keith and Sheila. Some of these people ask you to do projects that Sheila or Keith have requested of them. You want to be friendly and helpful, yet you also need to make sure you get your own projects done and that you're not agreeing to something unauthorized by Keith and Sheila. How do you handle this?

Outcome desired:

To keep a good working relationship and prioritize your supervisor's needs first. You also wish to be viewed as cooperative by your co-workers.

Other person's view:

They might just assume that you are free to do their projects also. Keith and Sheila may have told them they could check with you if you had free time. They might think that since their projects are for the same supervisors, they fall under a collective responsibility.

Best phrased:

If they are physically present with project in hand: "I would love to help you out. I am swamped with projects though and won't be able to get to it until Wednesday. Is there someone else that can help you, or should we see if Keith or Sheila would like to have me hold off on one of their projects in order to attend to this project?" Then visit Keith and Sheila together. If they are trying to just pawn off a project, they will likely say you don't need to bother the boss, and that they will find someone else to do it.

If this continues, then you need to get clarification of job responsibilities from Keith and Sheila. Approach them and say, "I want to be sure I do everything possible to make your jobs easier and I want to be accessible whenever you need me. I am getting almost daily requests by your people to do projects for them. Often I am swamped and would have to drop a project I am doing for you in order to do their project. I would say these projects currently take up about ten hours of my time a week. How would you like me to handle this? Should I check with you on each project? Should they check with you before handing a project to me?"

Keith and Sheila may be unaware that others on their staff are asking you to do so many projects. If they do instruct you to comply with requests for work on projects, then monitor your time on each project. That way if Sheila or Keith complain that you aren't getting to their stuff you will be able to accurately account for your time.

Situation:

You were hired sixteen months ago. You are still waiting for your one-year review. You feel slightly anxious to know what your boss thinks of your performance, and you are now four months past your scheduled pay increase. Your boss is very busy and keeps putting your review off. How do you handle this?

Outcome desired:

You want to get your raise and to know if you are performing as expected. If not, you want to be able to adjust so you can get a favorable review next time.

Other person's view:

Let's assume you have approached your boss on this but he keeps putting it off with assurances that you are doing just fine. Your boss probably is swamped and doesn't know how to deal with it. Your boss might not realize your pay raise won't happen until the review is done. Your boss needs and wants you to perform at your best. Your boss is not trying to keep money from you.

Best phrased:

"Tom, I know you are really busy and I want to be able to work as best as I can for you. The best way to serve you is to know what I do well and what areas you need me to take on. I would really like to find some time when we can go through my review. I also understand I need to have the review turned in before any pay change will kick in. What time looks best next week to do this?" Then be sure to pick a time and book a conference room.

Situation:

You have been working hard and feel you deserve a promotion. You are frustrated as you feel you are constantly overlooked. Recently Mary got promoted into the position you wanted. Who do you approach? How do you handle this?

Outcome desired:

You want to be promoted to the next level.

Other person's view:

Your boss may have just overlooked you. There may be things you need to work on, but are not aware of. There may be other reasons why Mary got promoted and you didn't. Management may have a different role in mind for you.

Best phrased:

This is tricky. Never go in comparing yourself to Mary or even asking why Mary got promoted instead of you. You will come off as a whiner. Instead say, "Bill, I would really like to get promoted. I want to find out from you what things you think I need to work on in order to be promoted to the next level. Could you also tell me which position I am likely to be considered for based on my abilities?"

This allows your boss to be open with you on what you need to work on. Make sure you have a positive attitude. I have seen many people with a positive attitude but only 60% skill get promoted over people with 90% skill and a negative attitude. The best way to make yourself promotable is to develop a positive way of looking at things.

Situation:

Your company is experiencing growing pains. There is more work than there are people to do the work. You work very hard and bring a positive attitude and energy to your job. Joy, who has a negative attitude, quits. A few days later she is back at work bragging she got a raise. How do you handle this?

Outcome desired:

You want to feel good about the work you are doing and not feel taken advantage of. You want to see people promoted because of qualifications, not because a warm body is needed nor because of a "squeaky wheel gets the grease" policy.

Other person's view:

Your company may be in a bind and simply need people. They may not have recognized her attitude because she might not show it around upper management. She may also be more skilled than you think. Your company wants happy employees and wants to be able to serve the customer.

Best phrased:

Approach to your boss: "Do you have a quick second to chat?" Staying upbeat you say: "I really like working here and I know there is a crunch time and we need people in positions. I'm confused about one thing and I hope you can put it in perspective for me. I have noticed that some people are quitting and then being hired back at a higher salary. I'm confused as to why and I'm wondering if it is affecting morale."

Just leave it at that and let the boss explain. Do not act defiant or suggest that you can just quit and get a higher salary. Inevitably top management will be comprised of people who are dedicated with good attitudes. Even if the boss doesn't really respond to you, you have made the point that it is causing a morale problem. This will prod them to look into it further.

Now your boss may become defensive and respond curtly. "Who are you talking about?" or "You just do the job you are hired for and don't worry about anyone else." Such responses tell you he is feeling challenged and pressured. You need to consider whether you want to stay in that environment. If you do, then say, "I'm not here to talk about anyone specifically. I'm only here because I know you want what is best for everyone and you want a productive working environment. I will continue to do my job well. My only intent was to get some clarity on the issue."

HOT TIP: If at anytime you feel attacked by someone and you are not prepared to respond, DON'T. Most likely you will say something you regret or else you will spend your whole time steaming that you didn't say what you wanted to. Instead say, "I can see that you are really upset and I do want to talk this over with you. I would like some time to collect my thoughts. Are you available to talk about this in ———(put in the time you need whether it is ten minutes or a day)."

Situation:

You're a department head. The vice president to whom you report seems to enjoy finding fault with your staff. He can be downright mean in his references to individuals—never pointing out their positive attributes. You feel it is a reflection on you and feel obligated to defend them from his criticism. How do you handle this?

Outcome desired:

You want your boss to recognize the positive contributions made by people within your department. You want him to see that you and your team do a good job.

Other person's view:

He might not feel you are managing them correctly. He might not even hear how negative he sounds. He might believe the area is unimportant overall. Or, he might just have a bee in his bonnet about this area. There is probably a hidden message here that needs to surface. Your boss could want you to institute changes or interact with your employees differently and doesn't know how to directly address it with you. Or your boss really does feel that your department is not working to its potential. Either way you need it clarified.

Best phrased:

Approach him with, "Ralph, I would like to take some time to talk with you about my area. Do you have thirty minutes to spare today?" Get on his calendar. At the meeting say, "Ralph, I really want to do a good job for the company and for you. I am confused when you consistently point out my employees' bad points. I am not sure if you feel that I am doing something incorrectly in my management capacity and want me to change, or if you feel that they can't do the work. I would really like to itemize the changes you would like to see in me and my department so we can be more productive. We would love to hear some positive feedback, and I'd like your input on how we can earn that." Then let him talk and air his feelings. Before you leave, clarify the points each of you made and reiterate what you heard you need to do in order to get your area recognized.

Situation:

The entire office is backlogged and everyone is working in crisis mode. Your supervisor keeps dropping in, but so far has not pitched in to help. You feel he should roll up his sleeves and dig in with everyone. How do you approach him?

Outcome desired:

You want your supervisor to pitch in and help out.

Other person's view:

He may have another project he's working on. You know he wants morale to be good. He doesn't realize how everyone is feeling overworked.

Best phrased:

"Joe, we are really swamped out here. I really think it would boast morale if you could lend us a hand. Or, maybe we could get some extra help? What are your thoughts?" If Joe is working on a project, this would prompt him to tell you and then get help. If he isn't working on any other project, it lets him know that the team needs his support.

Situation:

You are on the phone and someone stops at your cubicle. Your conversation is confidential, but the other person keeps looking in your cubicle or standing in your door. How do you handle this?

Outcome desired:

You want to have an uninterrupted conversation and you don't want it overheard.

Other person's view:

She might not think you see her so she stays in view. She might have something on her mind that she feels is urgent. She might be oblivious to proper etiquette and not know that she should walk away and come back.

Best phrased:

First of all, acknowledge the person. If you don't she will try even harder to get your attention. If you will be off in the phone in five minutes, look at the person, smile, raise your hand to indicate five minutes and then point to her cubicle. If she doesn't leave, wave good-bye. Then when your conversation is over, go straight to her cubicle. At that time say, "Sorry to keep you waiting but I had to finish that conversation. In the future, just peek in and if I'm in the middle of a conversation and can't be interrupted, I'll signal you and then when I'm free, I'll come right over to your office. If I'll be right off, I'll motion you in. If it's really urgent, jot me a note and hand it to me. That way I can respect your time. So, what can I do for you?"

Situation:

You are in an area where a lot of people congregate at your desk. You often return to find a pen, stapler or some other object missing, or you find things moved on your desk. You tend to be very neat so this bothers you. How do you handle?

Outcome desired:

You want your area kept neat and you want to maintain a good relationship with everybody.

Other person's view:

Many people just view the items as office supplies and don't get as attached to them as you do. Or, they don't even realize they are taking things from your area. They have no idea it annoys you.

Best phrased:

In a light, joking manner, say, "I realize I may sound weird about this, but humor me! I really like to keep my area neat. I know I'm in a high traffic area and my desk is a hand supply stop. All I ask is, if you use something, please put it back exactly the way you found it. I really appreciate you doing this for me." If you have too many people to tell, then anchor down the items that are most used, put your favorites in a drawer, and put up a cute sign that says, "Welcome. Go ahead and use anything, but please put it back right where you found it. The owner of this desk has been known to go wacko searching for items."

Remember: People extend their personal space to their office area. For some people, this means they make little "homes," complete with pictures, flowers, favorite mugs and the like. If you are like this, then you might feel like your personal space is invaded when people move things or take things. When they move things, it's actually like they are taking a piece of personal clothing off of you! Not all people feel this way. Many do not personalize their offices.

For some, you could walk into their office, put up someone else's nameplate, and no one would notice. We all tend to assume our quirks are universal.

Point out your preference in style in a light manner, otherwise others will think you are just being difficult.

Situation:

You feel people are not responding promptly to your calls, requests, faxes and/or e-mails. You feel very frustrated. You cannot complete your work in a timely fashion without the necessary input.

Outcome desired:

You want the information on time so you can proceed with your job.

Other person's view:

She doesn't realize the significance of what you need. She forgets or misplaces things. She's overworked and hampered herself by others' delayed responses.

Best phrased:

(For internal employees): State on top of the memo in bold writing—"In order to reserve a spot for this session, you must return this form to me by 10/21 at 2 p.m. If you do not respond, we will assume you will not be coming. You will not be able to attend if you do not RSVP." Let them know what the consequences are so you are not continually having to seek people out to get their responses.

(For customers): Make sure you are making it easy for them. If you need a response, print it in bold up front. Don't bury it in the memo. If there is a consequence, state that in a friendly manner—"In order to best serve you, we need the following from you by _____ (Put a specific date here. If you say 'within the week' they will not have a deadline in mind and will forget.) If we do not receive it by that date, we will be unable to process your paperwork, which would mean action on your request will be delayed. Please call if there is any problem getting this information to us by the above date. We would love to be of assistance."

Situation:

Someone has just asked you to do a last minute project for them again. You feel overworked as it is and do not see how you will have the time to get it done for them.

Outcome desired:

You don't want extra work as it will stress you out, and you know you cannot do a professional job in the allotted time. You want to be seen as cooperative.

Other person's view:

She might feel you are so efficient that you can handle anything. She might not realize how much you are juggling. This is especially true if you are a person that has a hard time saying "NO." She just needs her project done and she wants help. She wants her project done well as it reflects on her. She knows she's never organized enough to do things early, so she assumes everyone else works in crisis mode too.

Best phrased:

If it is a co-worker: "I would love to help you out, Sue. Unfortunately, I am swamped and would not be able to even get to it until next Thursday. If you want to take over and do this project for me (give them one of your projects), then I could do yours. In the future, if you can give me more notice, perhaps we could look at rearranging things so I can help out more."

If it is your boss: "Since everything that goes out of our office reflects on us, I really want to make sure I do a good job for you. For this project, I would like to quickly sit down with you and assess what things I am working on that you are willing to have delayed so I can get to this. For the future, I would like to know what you need from me to help us avoid last minute projects. My concern is that I don't rush through things for you."

Situation:

You have a colleague who continually comes by to just chit-chat. You feel it really disrupts your work and causes you to have to make up lost time later. How do you handle this?

Outcome desired:

You want to seem friendly yet you also want to be able to leave the office on time.

Other person's view:

He can juggle many thought fragments at once and has no problem with people interrupting him so he thinks nothing of interrupting you. He is chatty and flourishes when in contact with others. He has no idea he's causing you problems. He wants to be liked.

Best phrased:

First of all, don't ignore this person. It will only encourage him to intensify efforts to get your attention. Meet him on his territory so you can escape. Stop by his office or cubicle when it's convenient for you and say hello. Always end by saying, "Well, I better quit chit-chatting and let you get back to work." If he comes by your work area, stop and say, "I would love to chat, but I'm in the middle of something. Why don't we go to lunch, so we can visit uninterrupted."

This type of person usually feels the need to talk right at that moment so he will leave and find someone else to talk with. If you really do value the person, find an appropriate time to mention your concerns, "Jim, I really enjoy talking with you. Unfortunately for me, I haven't mastered the art of talking and working at the same time so I end up getting behind. Maybe we can schedule some lunches or breaks together so we can catch up and both be able to get our work done."

Situation:
Every time you go to the copy room you encounter a long line. It seems the copiers are constantly breaking down. You find this a great source of irritation and frustration in your day, but so far, Mary, the person responsible for the copiers, hasn't done anything about it. How do you handle?

Outcome desired:
You want the copiers to work properly so you can complete your work and send it off to clients.

Other person's view:
Mary might be unaware that the copier keeps breaking down. She might be on a tight budget and doesn't see how the company can afford another copier right now. She may be unaware of the wasted time and consequences such as lost clients due to things being delayed.

Best phrased:
First, do your homework so you can provide concrete numbers to support your complaint. Saying "The copiers are always down," or "I can never get my stuff copied" is too vague and sounds merely like a complaint. Plus, it's an exaggeration that will weaken your position. Come to Mary with facts and figures, saying something like: "Mary, I know we want to get things out to the customer as fast as possible. The copier keeps breaking down and delaying projects. It is down on average of six hours a week. What are your thoughts on getting another copier, or getting a copy company to do pick ups, make copies and return them the same day? I estimate right now that those six hours are costing us $250 per week in lost time. In a few weeks, it may be more cost effective if we had a new one?"

Leave the last line open as a question. Remember, there may be many other priorities in the budget of which you are unaware. Help the person who can fix the situation see how it affects the customer and the company, not just the employees.

Situation:

You are feeling minimized by others outside of your team. Answers you need and projects you need completed by others are consistently delayed, ignored, or incomplete. How do you handle?

Outcome desired:

You want all projects turned in on time so you can meet deadlines.

Others' view:

They are so focused on their job they don't see the relevance of what you need. Maybe jobs are in a crisis mode; everyone is just trying to get by. They too want to do a good job and help the customer.

Best phrased:

"Sara, in order to get documents out to our customers in time, there is certain information I need from you. I need to be able to get the answers back from you within twenty-four hours. What is the best way to touch base with you—phone, fax or e-mail? And is there anything you need from me in order to get it back quicker?"

Just try to brainstorm with her. You might be able to pass communications via computer. She may be so buried in work that the notes you send her are getting lost. There might be another place to access for information. Try to figure out the best way for both of you without causing a lot of extra work.

Situation:

You have been trying to contact Susan. You have left numerous messages, but have received no response. How do you handle?

Outcome desired:

You want to talk to Susan about an important matter, and you don't want to appear to be a pest.

Other person's view:

Maybe she knows she will be unable to accommodate your request so she doesn't see any reason to contact you. She is out of the office or on vacation. She is simply bad about returning messages. She may not want to deal with the matter and is avoiding it.

Best phrased:

When you leave voice mail be specific, "Hi Susan, This is Anne Warfield from Impression Management Professionals. I am just calling to touch base with you about_____(list what it is here). I will be in the office the rest of the day today. Thursday I will be available from 9-11:30 and then from 3 p.m. on. On Friday I will be in all day. I look forward to hearing from you. If I don't connect with you by Friday, I will give you a call first thing on Monday. Take care."

If someone really wants to talk with you, she will be grateful to know when she can get in touch with you. If she is avoiding you, then the above message lets her know she can't pretend to have called and was unable to reach you. It lets her know you will be back in contact, so your next phone call doesn't seem pesky. I recommend only leaving two voice mails. After that, don't leave any messages, just call again and again until you get a live person.

Situation:

It seems to take forever for change to occur in your company. You have some ideas on how to improve things. How do you handle?

Outcome desired:

You want the company to run smoothly and you want your job to be focused.

Other person's view:

Your boss may be overwhelmed. He might be stuck in a paradigm where the notion of change is foreign, i.e., "This is the way we've always done it." He might not have thought of any new ways to do things. He might not know how to implement changes. He wants to have the company run as profitably and smoothly as possible.

Best phrased:

"John, I have some ideas on how we can make this area even more productive. I'd like to bounce them off of you and see how we could implement some of them."

Get him to set aside some time. Ask him to comment on the pros and cons of your ideas. This would force him to look for the good points as well as the negative. If you want, tell him you will take responsibility to implement any changes if he gives you the authority to do so.

Whatever you do, don't approach him arrogantly, as if everything is now being done stupidly. You don't want to come across as a know-it-all and not a team player. Remember your body language—keep a neutral stance and use open hands.

Situation:

You made a mistake on the job. You do not realize your error. You do sense that another person, Tim, seems disgusted with the job you did. The next thing you know, Tim is in speaking to your boss. Later on your boss, Travis, stops to talk to you about your error. How do you handle?

Outcome desired:

You want Tim to come to you and not your boss. You don't want a rift between you and Tim and you want your boss to see your good points.

Other person's view:

Tim may have low confidence and doesn't feel like he can come to you. He may feed his self-esteem by pointing out other people's mistakes. He might not like confrontation. He wants to be viewed positively also. He doesn't know how you would react to criticism. He may be self conscious about criticizing you.

Best phrased:

"Tim, Travis just stopped by and pointed out an error in my work that you caught. Thank you for catching that. Since we both want to do our best, I would love it if you would come to me first with any errors that you catch. That way we can review what I should have done. Would that be possible?"

If Tim is going to your boss for self-esteem, he will get it by now being in a position to show you the ropes. If he is just shy about confrontation, you have given him reassurance there will be none, and that you welcome direct communication. And if he just likes pointing out mistakes, he knows he can't go around you because you will confront him again.

If it does happen again, confront him. "Tim, Travis just came and showed me another error. I thought we had agreed that you would come to me first, show me the error and allow me to correct it. What can we do so this doesn't happen again?" This lets him know you won't stand by meekly, yet your words and demeanor are cooperative.

Situation:

A co-worker in your area is slacking off. You notice that she's continually taking time off for personal business. This is affecting the department's morale. How do you handle?

Outcome desired:

You want good morale and you want the workload evened out.

Other person's view:

Maybe she has a lot going on in her life that you don't know about. Maybe she has pre-approval for the time off. Maybe the boss isn't aware of the amount of time she's taking off.

Best phrased:

This will depend a lot on whether you have a weak or strong boss. A weak boss will never want to confront the person and you may have to confront the person yourself. If you have a strong boss, simply ask for a private meeting. Then say, "Janet, I just wanted to talk with you about the area's morale. I know you really want your team to feel good about their work. There is one person that is taking a lot of personal time and it is really skewing the workload on to everyone else. Is there anything we can do about that?"

Now if the person has personal time off that the boss approved, Janet will tell you she is aware of it and that it's authorized. At that point, back off and be supportive. Maybe ask if it is possible to get in extra help. If your boss is unaware of the situation and wants to know who it is, state that you are not there to pick on anyone, you are simply concerned about employee morale. Then, identify the person. Be prepared for the boss to identify you as the source of the complaint.

Situation:

You feel as though a lot of decisions that affect your job are made by upper management without any input from those it affects. You are frustrated with this process. Recently the decision was made to institute a new paperwork form in your area. You feel it causes a lot of confusion and makes the process more difficult. How do you handle this?

Outcome desired:

You want your job to be performed in an efficient manner, with as little confusion as possible. You want to do a good job and have input in decisions.

Other person's view:

Management may think it is making very logical decisions. They are not trying to complicate people's lives. They want to run efficiently. They may have reasons for their decisions that you are not aware of. They would like to be productive.

Best phrased:

Approach your supervisor and say, "Do you have a quick second to chat about this new form? I'm not sure I know how to fill it out correctly or maybe it's just a confusing form. It seems that it is taking twice as long to work with customers. Can you share with me why we need to use this new form?" Try to just gather data. Your supervisor might not be aware of why things are being done the way they are. Find out who can give you the answers. Then approach your boss about being able to participate in more decisions. For example, "I know that decisions, like the new form, are made with the intent of making things easier. Is there any way we can have input in changes that will affect us? I realize how expensive printing new forms can be and I would like to be able to help make a form that will work right off the bat."

Situation:

You have a co-worker that's a chronic complainer. It is really getting on your nerves, especially since this worker seems to use his complaints as an excuse not to do his job. You are working together on an extra, last-minute project, and his constant complaining is extremely annoying. He is stretching your patience. How do you handle this?

Outcome desired:

You want to get through this project, keep your sanity and maintain a working relationship with this person. You don't want to listen to any more complaining.

Other person's view:

He might not realize he is complaining. He might think he's merely making conversation. He wants to be liked and respected. He wants to get along with his co-workers.

Best phrased:

You can use two different approaches. The first approach is to keep focusing on the positive side. Ask him what fun or exciting things have happened lately. If he complains about something, ask him to find something good about the situation. Keep doing this to steer the conversation to the positive. Or you can be direct and say, "Jack, in this whole time we've been chatting you have talked only about the negatives of this project. Tell me something positive. I need to hear good things to boost my spirits. All this negative talk can really get me down." Then let him talk.

Situation:

You like a quiet work area. You have a hard time concentrating with a lot of noise. Two other people with cubicles near yours blare their radios and talk loudly. How do you handle?

Outcome desired:

You want some peace and quiet when working. You want to maintain a good working relationship with your co-workers.

Other person's view:

Others can tune out the radio and not even hear it. They can concentrate in the middle of what to you is chaos. They don't realize it is annoying you. They want to get along with everyone also.

Best phrased:

The most important thing here is to be friendly and direct. Do not whine or complain. Instead simply say, "I really need quiet in order to concentrate and I have a hard time with the loud radios and the talking. Would you mind keeping it down just a little? I would really appreciate it." Then be sure to thank them the next day when they do keep it down.

If you have a good sense of humor you might preface your statement with a little self-deprecating humor, such as, "You know, when you're old and cranky the first thing that goes is noise tolerance." Or "Hey, just thought you'd like to know the U.S. Airforce base in Guam called to say 'Keep it down.'" "I guess I am more of a recluse than I ever thought! I would really appreciate it if you could keep the radio and talking down a little." Then thank them.

In The Workplace: Employees

Situation:

You want the employees to be informed. As their manager you ask Ben to sit in on some meetings, take notes, and report back to you. Your hope is that Ben will inform the others. You find that Ben will get the information, but still expects you to decipher his notes, transcribe them, and distribute. You find that this takes too much time. How do you handle?

Outcome desired:

You want Ben to take on the responsibility of informing everyone of the information that came from the meeting.

Other person's view:

Ben might feel he is stepping on your toes if he takes the initiative to disseminate his information without having your approval. He might think you wanted him only to sit in the meetings and take notes. He might feel awkward sharing the information with his peers—he may feel that doing so would be perceived as evidence he is "privileged." He might not want the responsibility of distributing the information.

Best phrased:

"Ben, you've been doing a great job attending those meetings and bringing back notes. Now, we need to develop a way to distribute the information to everyone. What are your ideas on how to do that?" Keep talking with him and see if you can get him to create a form, have a quick meeting or e-mail people with the information. Don't let him walk out without agreeing to complete the project. Make sure you end with something like, "Great Ben. Just so I understand, after the meeting you will write up a quick memo that outlines the key points and you will distribute the memo to everyone?"

Situation:

You promoted Annette to a new position. You know that Lucy has been wanting that position, but you don't feel she is ready for it. Lucy comes to discuss this with you. How do you handle?

Outcome desired:

Assuming Lucy is a good employee, you want her to keep working hard and to stay motivated.

Other person's view:

She is looking at all the years she has given to the company. She feels she is a good worker and that she is entitled to the promotion on the basis of her tenure. She doesn't understand what she needs to work on.

Best phrased:

"Lucy, I can see why you might be confused as to why you weren't promoted into the open position. I can also see you really would like to be promoted. Let's take time to review the key skills I see as necessary in ____(state the next open position here). Why don't we schedule some time tomorrow to go over this? I would like you to bring to our meeting a list of qualifications and strengths required by this position, and what strengths you feel you have, and what areas you feel you need to work on. Then we'll compare notes and devise a game plan."

If you don't believe Lucy has the appropriate attitude or skills to rise to the next level, then be direct about that. "Lucy, I can see why you would be frustrated, especially if you look solely at the years of experience you've put in. The most important quality I look for in a person for that position is a positive attitude. To me this means a person who is cheerful, looks for the positive in others, happily takes on projects and constantly looks for new ways to do things. I look for a person to be a real self-starter. In this last year I have given you two projects to work on. The first one you grumbled about and told me you thought it was unnecessary. For the second one, you did only what I asked of you and I kept having to spell out the next step. If you really are interested in moving up, then I would be happy to work with you on this. What are your thoughts?" Then be really direct about how they need to change: no complaining, taking initiative, being more resourceful, volunteering for projects. Be sure to coach and acknowledge any advances or improvements. You could even suggest a written list of traits they see in the people who work in the desired position.

If it is skills Lucy is missing then point out what skills she needs to develop and ask her how she would like to handle developing those skills. Let her manage you in this process since it's her career and she needs to be accountable.

Many people are either unaware of or confused about the degree to which they must be pro-active in securing promotions. They feel management should just see what they are doing and then promote them accordingly. They don't realize they need to take control.

Situation:

Much of your staff has been with you for a long period of time. You also have some new hires. Many of the long-time employees will try to stretch the rules as far as they can go. How do you handle?

Outcome desired:

You want peace, harmony and consistency in the office. You want everyone to feel accountable in their job and to stick to the standards you have set. You don't want to look like a tyrant.

Staff view:

They feel they have earned the perks. They don't see it as bad, just as bending the rules a little. They don't see how it upsets the order of the office.

Best phrased:

This one is tricky. No matter how you handle this, most likely the senior people will feel punished because their expectation to this point is that you will let it slide, because you have! You have two choices:

One is to make up a team to set the rules and submit them to you for approval. Once these are in writing, distribute them to everyone and it's a done deal.

Your second option is to call a meeting of the senior staff to talk about how they set the example. Enjoin them as allies and remind them to stick to the guidelines so that there's no misunderstanding of how the office runs. You might say, "I pulled you all together because I need your assistance. You have been here many years and over time we have all gotten lax on following the guidelines on vacations, etc. I have printed out for each of you our current guidelines. My dilemma is if I continue to let things slide like they have, our new staff members will get a mixed message as to what is acceptable. So I need for us as a group, to commit to sticking by these written guidelines from now on. It's the only way I can think to keep a consistent message to everyone. Does anyone have any other ideas?"

Let everyone talk and perhaps, a better idea will emerge. For example, one area might say they would like to keep the flexibility and will commit to always having all their work done on time. If that's the case, set strict standards for work done and stick to them. You might find employees in that area have hit on a great new policy for better productivity and enhanced job satisfaction.

Situation:

An employee under your supervision is chronically negative. No matter what you say, she always seems to say the exact opposite. Every job you assign to her seems to require so much effort. She does complete things in on time, but the negativity is getting to you. Her work is impeccable.

Outcome desired:

You want a pleasant office to work in. You want an atmosphere charged with the spirit of "I can" rather than "I can't."

Other person's view:

She doesn't see herself as negative, merely practical. She doesn't feel she is appreciated so she feels she must point out all she does, in detail, so you know how much work you are giving her. This makes her feel acknowledged. She wants some control and she feels this gives it to her.

Best phrased:

First of all, always acknowledge the work she does do. Let her know she is appreciated and then hold her accountable for her attitude. Say, "Renee, I want to take some time to talk about how we can ease some of the stress in the office. I am really impressed with the quality of your work. You are always very detailed and exact in all you do. I do get worn out with the negative way in which each project is approached. I feel like you might not see that I appreciate what you do, or that I am just giving you projects without realizing the details involved. I really want us to work in a positive environment where we both feel appreciated by each other. What can I do to make it easier to maintain a positive attitude at the office about projects?"

Then let her talk. Find out what she needs from you. Once it is agreed on then set up a plan of how you will each flag the other if things go off track. For example, let's say she tells you she feels rushed when you go over projects and doesn't feel you know what else she's working on. You might agree to touch base with her weekly so you are aware of what she's working on. Pause after you give her a project so she can ask any questions she may have. Remember to stay patient through this process. Agree to it and then say, "I will agree to slow down and answer any questions you have about a project I pass off to you and you will agree to be more positive about the assignments. If either of us gets off track, let's quickly point it out so we stick to this. Thanks, Renee."

Situation:

One of the documents sent to your clients went out with incorrect pricing on it. This is the third time this has happened in your area. You know that documentation is not completely systemized, yet you feel everyone should be checking all the documents thoroughly before they go out. You have addressed this before. You feel like you have to personally look everything over. You don't feel you have time for this. How do you handle this?

Outcome desired:

You want the correct documents to go out to clients. You don't want errors that should be avoidable in the first place. You want each person to accept accountability for their job and their mistakes.

Other person's view:

It is just a document and there are so many numbers on it. It isn't their job to proof this area. We had to rush to get it out. They feel they are doing the best they can under pressure.

Best phrased:

Call in the team as a group. "I know we can all agree that we want to deliver the best to all our customers. This means that we each have to be accountable for everything we do and to constantly look at everything with an eye toward delivering the best for the customer, whether or not a particular task is written in our job description. In the last three weeks we have had three documents go out with errors. The last one went to Pennlope Products and the error almost ended a fifteen year relationship. We have done $50 million in business with Pennlope and they were going to walk away from the account because of this. Now, I'm not here to point fingers and find out who made the error. So we don't have another document go out with an error, we need to start thinking as a team, constantly asking ourselves how we can make sure this doesn't happen again. So what ideas do you have to make sure this does not happen?"

List the ideas of the team. Make people accountable for all aspects of the area, not just their particular job. Encourage them to see that they must work as a team to do what is right for the customer. Watch the first three months and reward them for the changes.

Customer Relations

Situation:

You work in the Human Resource department. You notice more requests by clients for information on things such as sexual discrimination and workman's compensation as well as a few other requests. How do you handle the increased requests during your busiest time?

Outcome desired:

You want to service your clients while keeping your area organized during a busy time.

Other person's view:

The information is needed, and you have it. It is immaterial whether it is a good time for you or not. People trust you to get them the answers.

Best phrased:

First of all, this is perfect for the systemizing we talked about earlier. In this case, I recommend you put the answers in written form and organize them according to topic so you can fax answers to others who call. Until you get that completed, give clients an exact time by which you will have the information to them. "I will fax you the information on sexual discrimination by Friday at 4 p.m."

Situation:

On Monday, a client calls and requests a report they would like tomorrow. You know that with the amount of work on your desk, you can't get it to them until Friday. How do you handle this?

Outcome desired:

You want the client to be satisfied and not to feel you are brushing them off. You want them to recognize the delay.

Other person's view:

They need the information right away. They don't realize how swamped you are. They also want a good working relationship with you.

Best phrased:

"Miranda, I would love to get that report to you. I do want to give the report and your account the attention they deserve. If Friday is acceptable, I would be able to give it the time it deserves. Would that work for you?"

If this won't work, ask what information they need and why. Perhaps you can send them an abbreviated version. Find out if they need this for a specific meeting. Many times people want something yesterday simply because it occurred to them they should have it. But they don't really have a specific, immediate need for the material.

Situation:

You do contract work for a company. They love your work and want you to come back and do more for them, but they only want to pay a quarter of your fee. How do you handle this?

Outcome desired:

You want to keep a good relationship with them since they might give you referrals. You don't want to blow a chance to negotiate if there is an opportunity to do so.

Company's view:

There are other, less expensive contractors available. They might not realize the value of what you do. Or, they do realize the value but simply can't afford to pay you what you are worth.

Best phrased:

"Jenny, let me ask you this. You have built a great company that delivers the best in computer networking. If a client came to you, said you were the best and they wanted to use you, but they wanted to only pay a quarter of your fee, what would you do?" Most likely Jenny would say no she wouldn't take the job. Then just say, "Well, what would you do if you were me?" Most likely she will admit that, yes, she would have to turn down the job.

Reiterate that you know she understands the full value of what you do and ask her if there is any other way you can work together. Be creative with trade outs, payments, or retainer fees. Will they give a letter of recommendation of your work and give you their client list for mailings? Think beyond just the fee.

Situation:

You have worked hard on a client's project. They have continually delayed responding to your requests for information and have been very bad about returning phone calls. The project is off course and will take longer than originally projected. On top of that, they are making changes that now throw your cost way off. How do you handle this?

Outcome desired:

You want the customer to see you as cooperative and competent. You don't want to be taken advantage of.

Other person's view:

They might not realize they are being difficult. They may be prepared to pay more but you haven't brought it up. They want a good working relationship and the best product possible.

Best phrased:

"I realize things may have changed since we first started this project. I would like to take some time to reassess what we have done, and where you would like to go with this project. We should also revisit the cost since some of the changes you wish to make were not reflected in the first cost. With that in mind, let me know if you want to keep the changes or not. Also, let me know how you would like me to handle all changes in the future. Do you want me to fax them back along with the cost?" Once you have agreed to everything mention, "One thing that would really help the timing of the project is to be able to get an answer from someone within twenty-four hours. George, would it still be best to call you or do you have a back-up contact? Also are there other numbers or e-mail I can use to reach you?"

Family And Friends

Situation:

You've made a decision to move your parents into a Senior Living Complex. They are resistant to the idea. They are sad to be leaving their house and don't see why they need to move into this place. Your Dad has bad vision and can't drive. Your mother has diabetes and although she can drive, she shouldn't. You are concerned for their safety. They are angry. How do you handle this?

Outcome desired:

You want them to be safe. You want them to enjoy the new place they are moving to.

Parent's view:

They raised you in their house. To them they are giving up a part of their history. They have always been independent. They don't want to admit they need to rely on anyone. They don't want to feel old.

Best phrased:

"Mom and Dad, I love you. You have raised me to be responsible, to always do the right thing even if it isn't what I want to do. I believe in all the things you have taught me. I also know that for selfish reasons I want you around to talk to and be with. I watch you in this house and the amount of work it has become. I just want you to relax and enjoy yourselves. I know this house has a lot of memories and it will be hard for me to sell it also, but the house is only a small part of what we have as a family. I really think you will like this new place. I just need you to know I want you to be happy." Then let them talk about leaving the neighbors, the house and their present life style. For them it is a grieving period and you need to let them go through it in their own way.

Situation:

Diane always seems to have financial problems and is often asking you to loan her some money. She doesn't repay until you have reminded her many times. This frustrates you and makes you feel guilty.

Outcome desired:

You want to remain friends and be supportive of her. You don't want to lend her anymore money.

Other person's view:

She may have a more easy going nature and not take her borrowing seriously. She might forget who she owes what. She might be so embarrassed she hopes you forget she borrowed money. She wants to be your friend and doesn't want to make you feel bad.

Best phrased:

"Diane, I can appreciate that you are in a tight spot financially and need support. I will definitely be here for you in every way but financially. Having to continually ask for the money back really makes me feel like a heel and I know you don't want me to feel that way. So I think it is just best if we keep financial issues separate from now on." Then smile and go on to something else. Don't let her wheedle you back into doing it. If she pressures you say, "My parents always said to never loan money to anyone and I have broken that rule a few times. I have never had good success. I have now decided that no friendship is worth losing over money and will no longer lend money to friends."

Situation:

You have a teenager who is always late for family functions. Somehow he always makes it to his friend's events, or to hockey or basketball. Moreover, he never apologizes for being late. This really, really irritates you.

Outcome desired:

You want him to be on time for family events. If he must be delayed, you want him to call and then apologize.

Other person's view:

He might be really into his friends and might not see his behavior as disrespectful to the family. He is trying to spread his wings. He wants to be loved in his family.

Best phrased:

"Eric, I know this is a great time to be with your friends, and family might not seem as important. The family is important to me, and I need you to respect our family events; part of that means arriving on time. When you're late, it comes off as though you don't care about anyone but yourself. I know you don't think that way. We always make it a point to attend your events on time and we need you to do the same for us. So how can we make this happen?" Let him talk and then get a firm commitment that he will be on time. You might compromise and let him out of some events, but hold him to others. Whatever you do, don't just shake your head and accept it. Remember to treat him with the same respect you want. By adhering to your own standards in handling the situation in a respectful manner, your son has the benefit of example as well as instruction.

Situation:

It seems to you that the entire task of managing the household falls to you. You feel like your husband never plans meals and you have to juggle the kids, job, housework, cooking, laundry, and shopping. You are tired and cranky. How do you handle this?

Outcome desired:

You want your husband to pitch in and help with the housework. You want him to recognize the work you do and take on some of the planning.

Other person's view:

He doesn't think about food until he is hungry. He just wants to come home and play with the kids. He is fine having pizza every night. He doesn't realize that you make dinner every night. You hope he'll get the hint that you would love for him to make you dinner or take over the chores some nights.

Best phrased:

Talk to him at a time that is not tense or in the direct moment associated with dinner or housework. "Jake, I would love it if you would take some days during the week and plan the meals. I feel a lot of pressure when I have to work and then come home and try to think up a dinner to serve. Maybe we can alternate days and each be responsible for making dinner for everyone." Then make an agreement on dinner-time. If he does this, please don't complain if he makes the same meal each time he cooks. Instead, consider signing up for cooking classes and make a fun time of it. Bonus: you'll have regularly scheduled times to be together away from the house. Many men simply don't know how to cook, so it's not much fun. (Okay, so maybe we women don't either!)

Situation:

A friend constantly tells you what a great deal he got on his purchases. Whenever you buy something, he asks how much you paid for it. If you tell him, he immediately launches into a gleeful crow about the bad deal you made, with advice on where you should have bought it. This really gets on your nerves. Other than that, he is a great guy.

Outcome desired:

You want to remain friends. You want him to stop telling you about his bargains, and questioning your judgement on purchases.

Other person's view:

He really gets excited about getting a good deal. He wants his friends to get a good deal too. He doesn't think about how he is making you feel. He wants to be your friend.

Best phrased:

Next time he asks how much you paid for something say, "Charlie, when I tell you the price I paid for something, you tell me I got ripped off and that you saw it somewhere else cheaper. That really makes me feel bad. I like the deal I got, I like my lawnmower. Let's just talk about the mower. I know you're a terrific comparison shopper and when I need pricing info I'll be sure to come to you." Then start talking about the lawnmower and what it does. Often, a person who talks about price has no clue that he's making you feel as if you didn't make a smart purchase. He's just thinking about is how helpful he is with the information he has to share.

Situation:

Your friends started attending a church they really like. They constantly talk about it and want you to attend with them. You were raised Baptist and have no interest in attending their church. You are pleased that they like their religion, but almost dread going out with them because they pressure you so much.

Outcome desired:

You want to keep their friendship. You want to show them you are happy for them and you want them to respect your religion also.

Other person's view:

They are enthusiastic and just want to share their joy with their friends. They aren't perceiving this as pressure. They don't mean to put down your religion. They want to be friends.

Best phrased:

"Boy, you two sure seem so excited about your church! I think that's great. I really believe religion is important to each person and I appreciate that you want to share it with me. I am Baptist and like you, I really like my church. Although I appreciate your invitations, I won't be attending. But thank you. So tell me about...."

Then move on to another topic. If the church comes up again, politely listen and then change the subject. If they persist, "I thought I had expressed that I enjoy my church. I am not sure why you keep asking me to come to yours, when I already said no."

Situation:

You can't seem to do anything right in your Mom's eyes. She is constantly criticizing something: you don't get enough sleep, you don't earn enough money, you don't get enough recognition by your boss. This really wears on you. You know she means well, but you feel let down after you have been to visit her. How do you handle this?

Outcome desired:

You want to hear something positive from your Mom. You want her to keep her criticisms to herself. You want to enjoy your visits.

Other person's view:

She doesn't see herself picking on you. Instead, she sees herself being supportive of you and your endeavors. She thinks she is pushing you to do your best. She wants you to enjoy visiting her.

Best phrased:

"Mom, I love you and I know you believe in me. It is really hard to hear you always telling me I weigh too much, need more sleep or don't make enough money. When you do that, I feel like you think of me as a failure. I really like who I am and what I am doing. I just want you to celebrate with me about those things instead of focusing on my shortcomings. You are important to me and I want to share successes with you."

Let her talk. Every time from then on when she points out a negative be sure to stop her and say, "Mom, that wasn't a positive comment." Drop it and go on. Eventually the negative comments will stop, or at least they will be less frequent.

In Conclusion

Now What?

This is where the pavement hits the road. You have read the book and the difference it makes in your life is now up to you. How will you apply what you have learned? How are you going to practice it? Reading this book is just the beginning of your journey with your new way of thinking. The magical difference is going to come as you practice what you learned every day.

I recommend that you read this book every three months to check yourself on how well you're applying all parts of the Outcome Thinking™ philosophy. Challenge yourself! Ask yourself are you truly being positive in your thoughts? Try to see the best in every person and become more comfortable with who you are. Realize that your self worth comes from only you. Don't give that power to any other person.

I have seen Outcome Thinking™ help people get promotions, connect with lost family members, and get raises ranging from $5000 to $30,000. I have seen people become expert negotiators without being barracudas. I have watched clients move into management after they had been told they were not promoteable! I have watched marriages heal as people learn to focus on the other person. The bottom line is, I KNOW IT WORKS. Matter of fact, we have a excellent success ratio with people we personally coach. It is so gratifying to watch them make changes and see their progress in reaching their goals by using Outcome Thinking™.

Quite literally what you are holding is a key to a new relationship with other people. This is the key to great management, leadership, customer service, and sales. As with everything in life, you have to work hard to get the results you desire.

So I ask you to take this to heart. To always think, "How can I add value to this person?" "What is the outcome I desire?" and "How can I think and speak positively from the other person's perspective?" Believe the best in others. Concentrate on freeing yourself from right and wrong thinking. Stop worrying about what other people think about you and start focusing on connecting with others. Make people feel good and they will want to be around you.

So go forth on your journey. I encourage you to write down your thoughts in a journal. Catalog your successes so you can see your progress as you use your new skill. Be forgiving of yourself. Realize that it is going to take you a while to become fluent in your new skill. Take one step at a time, one thought at a time, one success at a time.

Best of luck on your journey!

About the Author

Anne Warfield, CSP, helps people develop the physical and mental image necessary to drive their lives and achieve their dreams. Corporations and associations across the country use Anne as a consultant, coach and speaker to discover how impression management can help them connect better with others and drive their business. Her customized interactive keynotes and programs—covering Outcome Thinking™, negotiating, body language, communication and presentation skills—entertain as well as educate.

With twenty years experience in impression management, Anne knows how it impacts business. She has used impression management to grow a $40 million dollar department as well as to run her own company. She has negotiated multimillion dollar deals in the United States and abroad. With twelve years in the image business, Anne knows what it takes to create a positive, lasting impression.

Anne has been awarded the CSP, the Certified Speaking Professional, by the National Speaking Association. This coveted designation has been granted to less than 10 percent of the speakers in the world.

Anne's expertise in impression management is constantly sought by television and radio stations. Anne is a member of the Minnesota Speakers Association and the National Speakers Association.

To inquire about booking Anne for your next program:

☎ Call: 888-IMP-9421 or 952-921-9421
📠 Fax: 952-921-9420
📧 E-mail: contact@impressionmanagement.com
🖥 www.impressionmanagement.com
or write:
✉ IMP, 7200 France Avenue S., Suite 224, Edina, MN 55435

Program Topics

....

For your next program consider one of the following dynamic, interactive customized programs:

- **Communicating More Effectively: I Know What I Said, But I'm Not Sure What You Heard**
- **Outcome Thinking™: Getting Results Without The Boxing Gloves**
- **Impression Management: How To Make 60 Seconds Count**
- **Success Negotiating: Less Stress, More Yes**
- **Spirituality In The Workplace: You Have To Go Inside To Be A Leader On The Outside**

All of these programs vary in length from 45 minutes to full day seminars. For more information on any of these topics or others please contact us at:

Impression Management Professionals
7200 France Avenue South, Suite 224
Edina, MN 55435
952-921-9421
888-IMP-9421
Fax: 952-921-9420
E-mail: contact@impressionmanagement.com
www.impressionmanagement.com